ALL-ITALY

ALL-ITALY

THE BOOK OF EVERYTHING ITALIAN

A QUARTO BOOK

RUNNING PRESS
BOOK PUBLISHERS
PHILADELPHIA, PENNSYLVANIA

A RUNNING PRESS / QUARTO BOOK

9 8 7 6 5 4 3 2 1

Digit on the right indicates the number of this printing.

Library of Congress Cataloging in Publication Number
86-042765

ISBN Paper O-89471-386-8

ALL ITALY: The Book of Everything Italian
was prepared and produced by
Quarto Marketing Ltd.
15 West 26th Street
New York, N.Y. 1OO1O

Editor: Felecia Abbadessa
Art Director/Designer: Mary Moriarty
Photo Research: Terri Binns and Karen Eisenstadt
Production Manager: Karen L. Greenberg
Layout: Alison Lee and Barbara Goodman

Typeset by I, CLAVDIA
Color separations by South Seas Graphic Art Company
Printed and bound in Hong Kong by Leefung-Asco Printers Ltd.

This book may be ordered from the publisher.
Please include $1.OO postage .
But try your bookstore first.
Running Press Book Publishers
125 South 22nd Street
Philadelphia, Pennsylvania 191O3

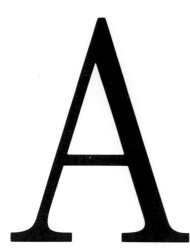UTHOR CREDITS

Frank Bianco: Cycling

Monica Gray de Cristoforis: Crafts

Gabriella Dosi Delfini: Film and Literature

Donald Flanell Friedman: Art; The Inventive Italians; Italian Comedy

Robert Holzer: Opera

Richard Horn: Interior Design

Nicoletta Iacobacci: Fashion

Arlene Isaacs: Travel

Francesca Manisco: Cuisine

Ada Francesca Marciano: Architecture

About the Authors

FRANK BIANCO is a freelance writer and photographer, whose articles and photographs have appeared in such publications as *Travel/Holiday, Sports Illustrated, The New York Times,* and other national publications. He and his wife, Marie, reside in Huntington, New York, within biking distance of Long Island University's C.W. Post campus, where he is a member of the Journalism faculty.

MONICA GRAY DE CRISTOFORIS was born and educated in Milan. After completing her studies, she worked as a writer, editor, and stylist for several popular Italian magazines. Most recently, she was an editor at *Abitare,* Italy's premier interior design magazine, where she wrote articles on interior design and decoration. She now works as a freelance writer for Italian magazines and periodicals in fashion, decoration, and design.

GABRIELLA DOSI DELFINI received her M.A. in Philosophy and History from the University of Padua. She has written for many scholarly journals on seventeenth- and eighteenth-century Italian history and culture. She is also the author of many articles on current topics for Italian women's magazines such as *Goia* and *Amica.* She lives in Milan with her three children.

DONALD FLANELL FRIEDMAN studied in Italy, France, Belgium, and Austria and received a Fulbright Fellowship before earning his Ph.D. in Comparative Literature from New York University. Several of his articles on art and literature have appeared in both scholarly and popular magazines and journals. He has contributed essays to *Arts* and his work has been included in several books. Donald Friedman teaches at Pace University and resides in Manhattan.

ROBERT HOLZER was born in Hackensack, New Jersey, and received his Ph.D. in Music from the University of Pennsylvania after receiving a M.A. in Music Theory from Rutgers University. He won an I.T.T. International Fellowship to study seventeenth-century choral music in Rome. He now works as a music editor for Garland Publishing.

RICHARD HORN has written extensively on design for such publications as *FMR, Architectural Digest, Gran Bazaar, New York, The New York Times, Metropolitan Home,* and *Metropolis.* His books include *MEMPHIS: Objects, Furniture, and Patterns* and *FIFTIES STYLE: Then and Now.* He has also published a novel, *DESIGNS.* Richard Horn lives in New York City and is currently the senior editor of *House Beautiful's Home Decorating.*

NICOLETTA IACOBACCI was a costume and set designer for Italian theatre and television. She is presently the news feature producer for R.A.I., the Italian radio and television corporation. Among other events, she has covered many fashion shows for R.A.I. including the Yves St. Laurent retrospective at the Metropolitan Museum of Art. She divides her time between New York and Rome.

ARLENE ISAACS has had many careers. She was trained as an opera singer, owned a Madison Avenue art gallery, and advised major corporations on their art collections. For the past several years she has been a travel writer and contributed articles to numerous magazines and newspapers such as *The New York Times, European Travel and Life, Travel and Leisure, Ovation,* and *Good Housekeeping,* among others. She lives in New York City.

FRANCESCA MANISCO is a freelance newscaster and producer for Italian television and radio. Her most recent production was "Women" a weekly radio program for the United Nations that was broadcast internationally. Born in Italy, she was educated in the United States and now lives in Rome and in New York.

ADA FRANCESCA MARCIANO obtained her M.A. in Architecture from the University of Rome where she currently works in the Department of Architecture and Urban Development. Ms. Marciano specialized in restoration at the International Centre for the Study of Preservation and Restoration and has worked on excavations at Ostia Antica, near Rome. Since 1978 she has worked with Professor Bruno Zevi, the renowned architectural historian, and on books by Einaudi, Electa, and other Italian publishers. She has written extensively on architecture for both trade journals and popular magazines. Currently she is the editor on the *Communicare l'Architettura* series written by Bruno Zevi.

Margaret Courtney-Clarke

ontents

Introduction

More people are visiting Italy than ever before; bent over guidebooks visitors trace the paths of Roman chariots to the tire tracks of Grand Prix Ferraris; they visualize the metamorphosis of leather thongs into Gucci loafers; and stand in an open piazza in the center of Rome, surrounded by a panorama of Renaissance palaces, Gothic churches, and baroque monuments—all of which rise as a testament to inspired artistry and heroic grace. Visitors meander through city streets, where life has flourished for centuries in the presence of a resonant, and unbroken cultural tradition.

In and around these historic scenes flow the vibrant and colorful sights and sounds of modern Italy. Sleek, sophisticated design, exquisite cuisine, superb craftsmanship, and avant-garde theater and art herald the energy and verve, the creativity and inventiveness of a vital contemporary society. Italy's incomparable allure is revealed in fusion of intellectual, emotional, and visual statements of the past and present.

To understand Italy's charm and influence, one must consider the centuries of history that have created this glorious country—one of the oldest in the West, the teacher of Europe, and the site and origin of great cultural epochs. Italy has always been unmistakable and brilliant. Since the ancient Etruscans first laid the foundations of what would become one of civilization's greatest empires, Italy has contributed most of the finest art, architecture, science, literature, and music known to the world. Every stone and statue, painting and song reflects a culture that is linked through its classical vocabulary to the language of today. A country that has never stopped influencing the rest of the world, Italy is as richly diverse as the tremendous treasures that are found there. To truly know Italy—her people, landscape, and culture—would require years of study of its complicated and lengthy history, which is recorded in countless books and documents; the Italy of past wars, treaties, alliances, kingdoms, papal states, and turbulent politics. But the real essence of Italy was born of the myths pirated from the ancient Greeks, the sensuous stories of Ovid and the heady romances that have enticed the hearts and imaginations of poets, artists, and lovers for centuries. This is the Italy of *dolce far niente* where it's sweet to do nothing but savor the simple, the earthy, and the sensual.

Literary accounts of Rome's founding are based both in mythology and history. There is the well-known tale of Romulus and Remus, who later grew up to found Rome in 753 B.C., the twins born of gods and raised by a she-wolf. Historians state that Rome was already a trading post in 509 B.C. when the Republic was established. Whether it was due to the divine fate of the gods, or the ingenious labor of human hands, the Republic flourished, and went on to conquer Carthage, Greece, Macedonia, and Egypt. Under Julius Caesar Rome extended its boundaries to Gaul, England, and Northern Europe. The assassination of this great emperor marked the beginning of the end of the Republic.

Following the decline of the Roman empire, Italy became Europe's battleground for many centuries, unable to unify its city-states against foreign intruders. Despite the ever-present specter of invasion and instability, Italy was the mother of the Renaissance and nurtured some of the greatest minds the world has known. During the Renaissance, the astronomer and physicist Galileo proved Copernicus' theory that the planets revolve around the sun; Leonardo da Vinci theorized that man could fly; the most profound works of Italian literature were written by Petrarch, Dante, and Boccaccio; and the pioneer of Italian unity, Niccolo Machiavelli, wrote his classic and controversial political treatise, *The Prince*. The visual arts also flourished during this period. Young Michelangelo illustrated the struggles of the human spirit through the marbles he carved, and under the auspices of Pope Julius II, he painted the ceiling of the Sistine Chapel, which remains one of the most sublime pictorial accomplishments in the world. The Renaissance heralded the beginning of a new world as seen through the cultural achievements in art, science, trade, and education.

Italy would not know official unification until 1861, when King Vittorio Emanulle and Count Cavour established the Kingdom of Italy. It took another decade of fighting against the Austrians to annex Venice, and Rome finally became the capital of Italy in 1870 when the Pope retreated to the Vatican State.

Today, Italy is the teacher of many arts, and supports an astounding variety of crafts and skills rarely practiced in the modern world. Artists and musicians from all over the world study here, living and working in the grand academies. Smaller contributions to everyday life include such well-known items as blue jeans, gelato, Roman candles, pizza, and Parmesan cheese. Through the years, Italians have taught poetry to the English, military arts to the Germans, cuisine to the French, acting and ballet to the Russians, and music and art to the world.

It would be very difficult to categorize the Italian people and speak of inclusive national characteristics. The country's physical terrain has always divided Italy into distinct and diverse regions; the north and the south are two separate entities much as England and Scotland are in the United Kingdom. A Roman is quite different from a Neapolitan. Florentines are known for their quick wit and sharp tongues; Neapolitans for their imagination; Milanese for their entrepreneurship; Piedmontese for their dignified, distinguished, reserved air. If national traits were to be ascribed, however, they would suggest an openly warm and affectionate people who are sensitive to art and beauty and are creative, inventive, social beings whose time is spent enjoying life to the fullest.

Even though the Italians are a diverse people, there is an underlying unity created by their strong pride and respect for the individual, and their sense of belonging to a community—a chain of life. No other aspect of Italian life is as highly revered as the family. It is this concern for family and community, as well as a genuine interest in foreigners, that makes the Italians a very hospitable and receptive people. Italy has always welcomed visitors, and visitors have gladly journeyed there.

The Roman ruins and their rustic surroundings have inspired many writers, particularly the Romantics. The poets from England stormed the sunny coasts of Italy as well as its cities and northern lakes; theirs are some of the best descriptions of eighteenth- and nineteenth-century Italy. Percy Bysshe Shelley wrote "Thou paradise of exiles, Italy!" before he drowned off the coast of Viareggio. The house in Rome where the immortal John Keats died in 1821 is now a museum with memorabilia of Shelley and Byron. Stendhal (Marie Henry Beyle) wished the following epitaph for his tomb: "Henry Beyle, Milanaise." He retired to Italy after the defeat of Napoleon and lived there until 1821. It was in Paris that he began work on *The Charterhouse of Parma*.

Verona was home away from home to such composers as Wagner and Mozart, and the poets Goethe and Heine. The greatest playwright in the English language, William Shakespeare, drew on Italy for the setting of several of his plays: *Romeo and Juliet, The Two Gentlemen of Verona* and *The Merchant of Venice.* Fanny Burney, English novelist and diarist, wrote, "Travelling is the ruin of all happiness! There's no looking at a building after seeing Palladio...!", the fifteenth-century architect whose style inspired George Washington's house in Mt. Vernon and Thomas Jefferson's Monticello.

In *ALL-ITALY* one will find a better understanding of this rich and glorious culture, a culture that continues to dazzle and delight us and to instruct most of Western civilization. Dr. Samuel Johnson had it right when he said, "A man who has not been in Italy, is always conscious of an inferiority."

Chapter 1

Interior Design

Above: Minimal, sleekly elegant yet thoroughly functional, this stool epitomizes what's best in mainstream contemporary Italian design.

You do not have to spend much time in Italy to realize just how much emphasis is placed on the visual aspect of things there. Perhaps part of it stems from the formality of Italian life, from there always being a "certain way of doing things," whether it is a question of dining, dressing, doing business, or socializing. Some of the specifics of that "certain way" may change from generation to generation. Other aspects of it might constitute unquestioned traditions. Whether of older or more recent vintage, these social forms remain a determining factor in daily living, and seem to have a visual equivalent in the carefully composed look of things Italian.

Perhaps the emphasis on the visual also stems, in part, from the fact that Italy has for centuries been imbued with the spirit of Catholicism, a religion notoriously rich in visual imagery. Consider the architecture of Italian churches, the rich vestments and accoutrements that heighten the spiritual and theatrical quality of sacred ceremonies, or the legendary lives of such Italian holy men as St. Francis of Assisi and his followers, recounted in the *Fioretti*, and overflowing with vivid miracles.

There is yet another factor that ought to be taken into account: The famous Italian sensuality that

Expect the unexpected with contemporary Italian interiors: in this case, a floor enhanced by a tangram-like puzzle pattern and the graphic, overscaled image of a bird in flight.

Left: Plaster walls steeped in a rich, brilliant blue capture the Italians' love of sensual surfaces and vivid colors. The walls also exemplify that traditional Italian crafts such as plasterwork are still practiced and appreciated today.

delights in all things that can be savored by touching, tasting, hearing, smelling, and last but by no means least, seeing. Whether this sensuality harks back to the days of ancient Rome, or is the flip side of Catholicism's strictures against physicality and sexuality; whether it simply grows out of an interest in the quality of daily life, or whether it is a combination of all of the above, the fact remains that Ital-ians have always been noted for their attention to sensuous detail.

Given all this, it is not surprising to find that interior design in Italy has been developed to a high degree of sophistication. Yet up until the 1960s, it would be hard to talk about a *specific* Italian approach to interiors. Until the sixties, Italy, whether it originated designs or adopted them from those of other nations, was comparable in its approach to decorating to the rest of Europe. Since the Renaissance, interior design had revolved around the conventionalized and quite rigid vocabulary of classicism. The classical model prevailed in interior design throughout Europe, or at least in the design favored by the upper echelon of European society. While the lower classes of each country developed their own design vernacular, the official history of interior design recognizes classical design as *the* basis for styles of decor. Whether the country in question was Italy, or France, or England, or Spain, the building blocks of the classical style—the column, the pediment, the various orders, the conventionalized ornamentation, and so on—were the essential elements of architecture, interior decoration, and furniture design.

Of course, there were national variations in the way the classical design vocabulary was employed: in the skill and care shown in the craftsmanship, in the materials used, and in influences from countries outside of Europe (for example, the oriental influences upon Venetian design, or the Moorish influences on Spanish design). Furthermore, the classical model *itself* was varied, and fancifully exaggerated into styles such as the baroque and the rococo which, while by no means classical, adhere to many notions of classical ordering. All the classically derived styles—Renaissance classicism, baroque, rococo, neoclassicism, the historical revivalism of the nineteenth century—were experienced throughout Europe. While each country expressed each style in its own particular way, there were strong family resemblances between all these expressions.

Today, things are quite different. There *is* no one reigning interior design style, in Italy or anyplace else. Democracy, electronic communication, widespread dissemination of information, late capitalism's reliance on planned obsolescence, constant shifts of fashion, and cultural polyphony have allowed for a more individual approach to design.

Nowhere has this individualism been so highly cultivated as in Italy. Its consumer elite has devel-

Right: Traditional pieces stand out with sculptural clarity in a pristine interior whose subtly proportioned volumes bespeak the fact that, in Italy, interior designers are trained as architects.

Left: This contemporary bench, designed by Achille Castiglione, gives some idea of how today's Italian designers are taking traditional pieces of furniture, such as this nineteenth-century garden seat, and using them as models for inspired updated versions.

Below: Strong horizontals and the sofa's light look, which is due to its being raised several inches off the floor, combine with the leather upholstery to create a sleek look. Contours are molded to the body, and the adjustable back and arms make this piece that much more pleasurable to lounge in.

oped an approach to interior design that, while lacking ironclad rules, is distinctly Italian in the exquisitely sensitive way in which disparate materials and styles of both the past and the present are brought together. The Italians' secret lies to a great degree in their ability to spot surprising affinities between the most seemingly diverse furniture, furnishings, materials, and proportions. True, such linkages characterize all eclectic interiors. Yet the kind the Italians create are often the least heavy-handed and obvious, and the most quirky and witty.

While examples of this approach can be pointed out easily enough, it is more difficult to pin down the logic behind them. Why, say, does a particular kind of wood flooring, with a particular sort of oddly shaped 1950s Italian armchair, upholstered in a particularly tangy viridian fabric, with a particularly cool silver-gray marble, with a particular *fin-de-siecle* Viennese table placed in the room in a way no *fin-de-siecle* Viennese would have placed it, with a particular kind of metal shelving—why should all this produce so enchanting an effect? Language is too logical to explain this, for the process of bringing it all together seems to owe more to instinct than logic. Perhaps it has everything to do with the Italian genius for subtle, delicious combinations (a genius, incidentally, that would have had much less of a chance to show itself in earlier, less markedly eclectic interior design styles, which permitted less freedom in terms of acceptable combinations).

In the captions that accompany the pictures in the following chapter, I will attempt to draw attention to various ways in which these contrasts work in the various types of interior design now current in Italy.

Memphis/Milano, Italy's leading avant-garde design group, is known—among many other achievements—for its experiments with vivid, Pop-inspired patterns. The experimental nature of their work is evident in the high-energy design of the carpet in this interior which was designed by Beppe Caturegli. The lower section of the large storage piece in the left-hand corner was designed for Memphis/Milano by George J. Sowden.

Memphis

Surely the most widely discussed feature of 1980s Italian design is Memphis/Milano, the Milan-based design collaborative. Founded by Ettore Sottsass, Jr., it offers his own furniture, decorative objects, fabrics, and plastic laminates, and those of a core group of talented young Milanese designers. There are also contributions from a number of architects and designers from various other countries, including the American architect Michael Graves, the Austrian Hans Hollein, and the Japanese Arata Isozaki. Sold throughout Western Europe and the United States, these pieces have gotten lots of attention from the media and exercise a strong influence on contemporary design the world over.

Distinguished by a wide range of colors (some extremely bright, others dull in a deadpan sort of way; some intentionally cold, others intentionally cloying); by materials and forms that simultaneously evoke popular suburban, ancient, and exotic cultures; and by production techniques that rely on both up-to-the-second technology and age-old craftsmanship, Memphis is a bundle of contradictions that resolves into some of the most extraordinary designs within recent memory.

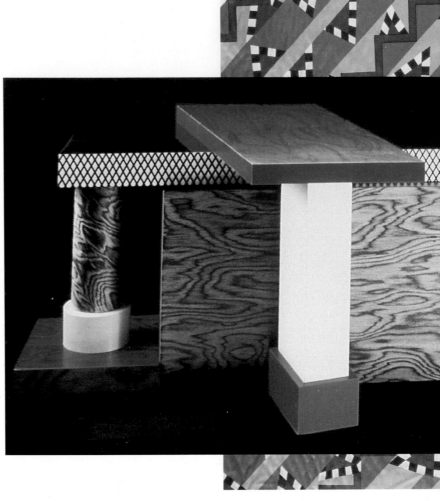

Memphis, despite its playful air, arose from a typically Italian tendency to view designs not merely as consumables that fulfill particular mundane functions, but as visual expressions of theoretical discourse. Specifically, Memphis/Milano's designs address certain, perhaps irresolvable contradictions in today's world, contradictions between high and low culture, between the rational and the irrational, between an object's functional and spiritual qualities, between permanence and obsolescence.

While European design movements throughout the twentieth century have come complete with manifestos and elaborate intellectual underpinnings, none have presented furniture and furnishings as a mode of theoretical discourse quite so emphatically as the post–World War II Italian design avant-garde. As Ettore Sottsass himself has put it, "We like words." Indeed, Italian designers, architects, and artists have liked them since the Futurists who, beginning in the teens and throughout the twenties, issued numerous manifestos defining their view of the world. They explained (if not always very clearly) how they would convey that world view in the plastic arts.

Apart from this Italian passion for design rhetoric, there may be other factors that strengthen the link between design and theory. With the onset of the Industrial Revolution in the early- to mid-1800s, the design process became more complex. Previously, for example, one craftsman designed, made, and sold, a table. Mechanization changed that. More and more people became involved in the processes of design and production. Furthermore, these processes were broken down into various steps, with different people assigned to each one. Methods of

Above: Matteo Thun designed this suspended, comic-book-inspired porcelain lighting fixture for Memphis/Milano.

distribution and sales, too, grew more complicated. The result, more often than not, was mass-produced designs of low quality.

By the beginning of the twentieth century, and particularly after World War I, a coherent design theory—not only in Italy, but throughout the rest of Europe and in the United States—was thought of as one way of controlling and coordinating the many specialized processes that went into the manufacturing of an object, and thereby improving the quality of mass-produced goods. Such improvement was hoped for, not

merely because it would result in more attractive, more saleable objects, but because it would in some way also improve the quality of life itself.

After World War II, when Italian intellectuals were intent on forging a new society out of the ruins of fascism, designers clung all the more fiercely to the belief that good design could help to better society. And so, during the 1950s and on into the early 1970s, design theory became not only a theory of how to design, but a theory of how to better the world—or if not better it, at least respond to it. Italian

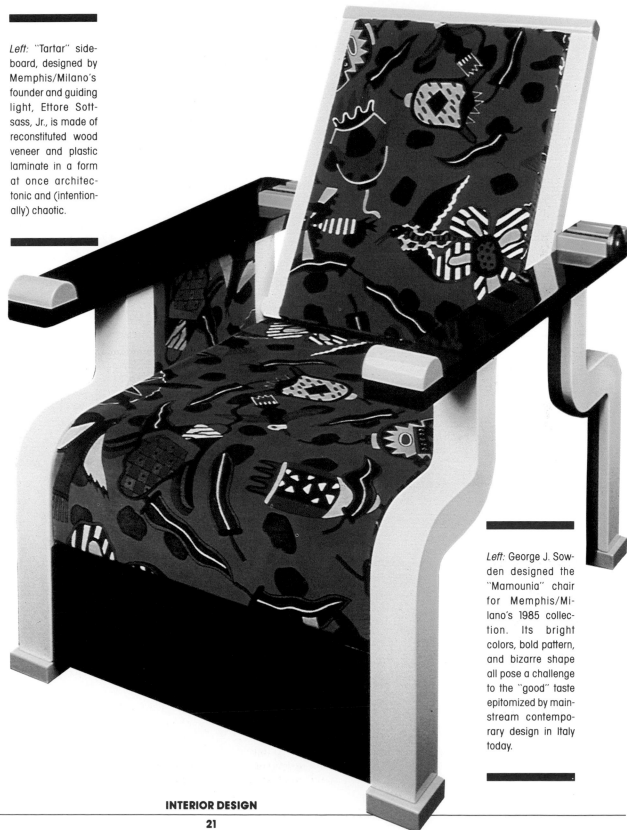

Left: "Tartar" sideboard, designed by Memphis/Milano's founder and guiding light, Ettore Sottsass, Jr., is made of reconstituted wood veneer and plastic laminate in a form at once architectonic and (intentionally) chaotic.

Above, underlay: "Cameroon," a cotton chintz created for Memphis/Milano by Nathalie du Pasquier, reflects the influence of African textile designs on her work and simultaneously recalls the American suburban landscape.

Left: George J. Sowden designed the "Mamounia" chair for Memphis/Milano's 1985 collection. Its bright colors, bold pattern, and bizarre shape all pose a challenge to the "good" taste epitomized by mainstream contemporary design in Italy today.

INTERIOR DESIGN

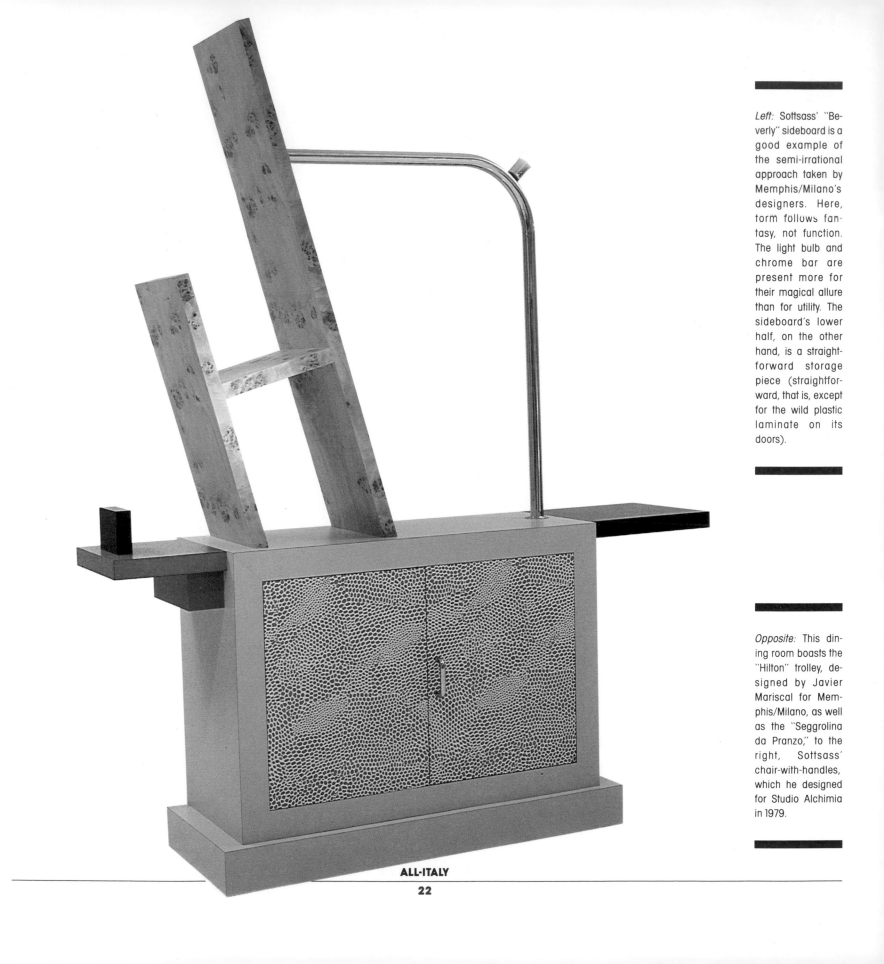

Left: Sottsass' "Beverly" sideboard is a good example of the semi-irrational approach taken by Memphis/Milano's designers. Here, form follows fantasy, not function. The light bulb and chrome bar are present more for their magical allure than for utility. The sideboard's lower half, on the other hand, is a straightforward storage piece (straightforward, that is, except for the wild plastic laminate on its doors).

Opposite: This dining room boasts the "Hilton" trolley, designed by Javier Mariscal for Memphis/Milano, as well as the "Seggrolina da Pranzo," to the right, Sottsass' chair-with-handles, which he designed for Studio Alchimia in 1979.

designers viewed their work as having not only aesthetic, but social, political, economic, and philosophical implications.

That a chapter on Italian interior design includes a section on Memphis/Milano is in some ways inappropriate, insofar as there *is* no real Memphis interior design. Because its designs have been conceived to make a splash as much in print as in practice, they have a strong, graphic quality well suited to photography, as if they would be best appreciated in isolation rather than as elements integrated into an interior. It has been said that Memphis/Milano's designers never conceived of all-Memphis rooms in the first place. Rather, they hoped that individual pieces would be incorporated into rooms decorated in a range of styles. Any all-Memphis rooms that have been seen were usually created for display purposes. Their high-energy play of super-vivid colors and hyperactive patterns would probably make them unpalatable to most people. Throughout this chapter, in the most diverse interiors, you will see a few Memphis pieces putting in an appearance. This is how most Italians now use them, if they use them at all—by mixing them in with other designs. The interiors shown here can be seen more as radical inspirations for living spaces than as actual places for people to work or live in.

Initially thought of by cynics as either a one-shot publicity stunt or an avant-garde phenomenon whose influence would prove short-lived, Memphis is now turning out to be an important force in Italian design today. Its focus in pattern and color, especially, seems to be affecting the work of more mainstream designers, and no doubt will be a determining factor for Italian design of the late 1980s and 1990s.

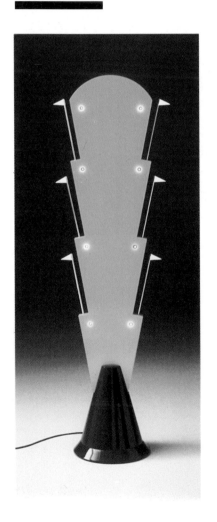

Studio Alchimia

Less well-known than Memphis, Studio Alchimia is another component of today's Italian avant-garde design scene. In fact, the two have the same roots in Studio Alchymia (note the slightly different spelling), a design collaborative founded in the late seventies, in which many ideas for a communicative, magical, oppositional design combining industrial methods and handcrafting were first advanced. A parting of the ways occurred due to differences of outlook and temperament, which lead to the development of two parallel groups.

Studio Alchimia's key figures are Alessandro Guerriero and Alessandro Mendini. In addition to designing furniture, objects, and interiors together along with numerous other designers, Mendini himself edits *Domus*, a beautifully produced, intelligent, and influential Italian design magazine, and collaborates with theater artists on performance pieces. Working with Bruno Gregori, Mendini has created for Zabro a collection of curious-looking furniture, including tables and storage pieces which hark back to art deco designs of the 1920s, yet at the same time have a strangely up-to-the-minute air about them. Many of these are

Below: Mendini and Gregori designed these pieces for Zabro's "Nuova Alchimia" collection. They are decorated with a colorful, almost funky pattern that ties them to Pop design. However, the fine craftsmanship in these pieces roots them in the tradition of Italian furniture making.

partly handcrafted and distinguished by superb inlay work, hand-painting, scagliola, and hand-worked wood and metal. At the same time, they might also show evidence of advanced technological processes. As compared to Memphis designs, these so-called "post-industrial" pieces, many of which boast polychromatic painted decorations reminiscent of the forms found in the 1920s and 1930s paintings of Wassily Kandinsky, have much less of a pop, cartoon-like quality to them. They are calmer, gentler, and quieter. They are also frankly elitist. In their elitism, these pieces bespeak Studio Alchimia's—and especially Alessandro Mendini's—approach to the present-day world, an approach that amounts not so much to an ironic acceptance, but to a heroic, perhaps slightly contemptuous defiance. Like Memphis' designs, these have a dreamy quality. Unlike those designs, Studio Alchimia's make a point of banishing suburban "tackiness" from any dreams they might inspire.

Studio Alchimia's interiors are no less extraordinary than its furniture. They are effectively akin to surrealist environments. In his book *Postmodern*, Italian architect and critic Paolo Partoghesi describes one interior as being "scattered with a series of oval openings connected by classical festoons. In each of the ovals a real mouth could be seen, belonging to a person hidden in the wall cavity." Other interiors feature subtle, slightly grotesque yet at the same time fascinating exaggerations of what Mendini calls "banal design"—essentially, Italian kitsch. Then there is his visionary "hermaphrodite architecture," in which Mendini seeks to combine formerly dominant, "masculine" architecture with formerly passive, "feminine" decoration,

bringing them together with an equality he might hope to see duplicated in society (or, perhaps, expressed within the same individual). In such rooms, Mendini writes, one could happen upon, "the deadened sounds, the twilights, the smells, the memories, the fabrics, scrolls, caresses, fluids, hiding places, the flowers, the grilles, cobwebs, pink colors, the tiny things, glass bells, microenvironmental involvements," which bring to mind the imaginary alternative worlds that the late Italian author Italo Calvino created in *Invisible Cities*.

Above: Mendini and Gregori created this table-chair for "Nuova Alchimia." The pattern on the back is typical of the way Mendini and his collaborators update and ironically twist visual motifs derived from early twentieth-century artistic movements.

The Sleek Look

Throughout the 1960s and 1970s, Italian interiors and home furnishings were considered the last word in sleek sensuality. Ever-widening industrial capabilities, development of new materials (especially plastics), and the willingness of designers to create with these new capabilities and materials in mind, while working closely with manu-

their orientation, are trained as architects. Pattern and decoration were often absent, as were rich, unusual color combinations.

The sense of speed conveyed by 1930s American streamline-style design and the "organic" curves characteristic of the furniture of the Finnish architect Alvar Aalto and the American designer Charles

facturers, contributed to the allure and resounding success of mainstream contemporary Italian design.

Insofar as the furnishings went, there was an emphasis on horizontal lines, voluptuously curved volumes, clear-cut shapes and mobility and flexibility. This is not surprising in a country where nearly all furniture and interior designers, no matter how *outre*

Eames captured the imagination of Italian designers immediately after World War II. As the Italian furniture industry started growing in the postwar years, these were the models to which designers looked when creating useful, everyday objects. At first, many of these objects were made by craftsmen as one-of-a-kind or limited-run items, in keeping with traditional Italian modes of production. Even-

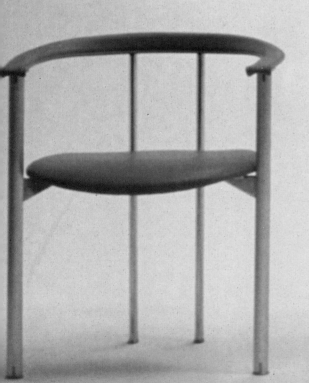

tually, though, they were mass-produced, as Italian manufacturers started learning from the precepts offered by efficient American industrialization and mass-marketing techniques. By the late 1960s, the sleek look of Italian design was known all over the world as the ultimate in consumer delights. In the typically

holds its own in everything from sofas and chairs to bathroom fixtures. Memphis and Studio Alchimia may be the most arresting features of Italy's design scene, but in most people's minds, Italian design still means opulently proportioned, leather-upholstered sofas; marble cocktail tables; gracefully zoomorphic lamps of

Italian refinement of their forms and the sensitivity shown to industrial and, especially, natural materials, these pieces far surpassed the Scandinavian and American originals which first inspired them, and become the furniture equivalents of the Ferrari.

While post-modernism's current reassessment of decoration is as evident in Italy as it is everywhere else, the look of sleek sensuality still

metal, stone and/or glass, often fitted with a tiny halogen bulb (perhaps the most notable technological development in Italian design of the past decade); brightly colored, plastic-handled doorknobs, faucets and taps; crisp, efficient kitchens composed of built-in-looking modular storage units in black, white, or soft pastels accented here and there with some bright, pure tone; coolly

Below: With the simplest design, this chair manages to take on a strong presence of its own. Its back, though no more than a thin strip, is molded to fit the back perfectly. In one of today's Italian interiors, this piece, because of its timeless styling, is as likely to be used with contemporary designs as it is with more traditional ones.

geometric tables in natural or lacquered wood; and elegant ceramic tiles. Less polemical than Sottsass or Mendini, and more interested in creating objects that will sell, the designers of these furnishings—including Marco Zanuso, Paolo Piva, Angelo Mangiarotti, Vico Magistretti, Gae Aulenti, Giovanni Offredi, Afra and Tobia Scarpa, Enzo Mari, DePas D'Urbino Lomazzi, and Antonio Citterio—are among the most well-respected names in contemporary Italian design, and the most responsible for forging its image: that of a super-sophisticated technology merged with natural materials in creations of inviting sumptuousness and modern sleekness.

The forms that this furniture takes are strong, so that the pieces themselves are often set in spare, airy interiors. To American eyes, these interiors look somewhat stark, yet they do not strike Italians in the same way, accustomed as they are to cool, sparsely furnished rooms well-suited to Mediterranean temperature highs, and familiar with the kind of grandly proportioned Renaissance pallazzi interiors in which furniture would have been kept to a minimum. Further visual interest is provided by the rich textures of the various materials used, artwork hung on the walls, and by the play of natural light in the room by day and electric light coming from strategically-positioned fixtures by night. The result might be thought of as sensual minimalism. Unlike more intellectual Italian design movements, the spirit that informs these interiors is rather hedonistic, and perhaps even a bit smug in what its detractors might call a bourgeois sort of way. But its appeal is much broader than that of the intellectual design movements, and it remains something to which many Italians strive today.

Below: Paolo Piva's "Alanda" sofa, designed for B&B, boasts an adjustable back and arms. In this pared down interior, the sofa seems to float in midair. Note the "important" portrait on the wall; juxtaposing it with the far more up-to-the-minute furniture is a typically Italian design ploy.

Stripped-Down Classicism

A variation of sleek Italian minimalism comes in the guise of a stripped-down classicism and/or neo-classicism. In these rooms also, furnishings are kept to a minimum. If the room is large enough, furniture might be placed quite close to the wall, as pieces were in both grand Renaissance interiors and the formal, aristocratic Italian interiors of the eighteenth century. Or else a piece of furniture might be allowed to float free of the walls, positioned in space like sculpture so that it might be viewed from all angles. The effect is not entirely welcoming, but rather one of breathtakingly austere chic, in mood not unlike some of the interiors glimpsed in Bertolucci's film, *The Conformist*.

Colors are low-key—grays, gray-greens, earth tones, and neutrals—and patterns are absent. The actual furniture consists not of sleek-lined, opulent contemporary designs, but of severe classical ones that are either antiques or present-day Italian reproductions or reinterpretations, made of natural woods, stone, or metal in classical or neoclassical designs.

In the rooms like these, particular attention might be paid to the walls and ceiling. If they are old, beautifully proportioned rooms,

Inset, top right: A minimum of furnishings, splendid materials, and perfectly proportioned details are an aspect of traditional Italian interior design that still finds favor today. This approach to design is evident in renovations of existing spaces as well as in newer interiors, which use older rooms as models.

Right: Delicately frescoed walls give this interior a haunted, out-of-time quality. The draped furniture emphasizes the effect.

moldings, friezes, and other surface ornamentation might be brought back to their former splendor. The walls of newer rooms, while kept bare of ornamentation, might boast a handsome, expertly applied coat of plaster steeped in some rich but subtle hue—this, an opportunity for the plaster worker to show off his skill with traditional finishes that might be linked to the particular region where the home is located. As for floors, they would be bare, and of either wood or—even more effective—terrazzo, marble, or some other stone. Artwork in such interiors might sound a contrastingly up-to-the-minute note; or else it will be some marble bust up on a plinth, a survivor from Roman times; or a vast tapestry with a mythological or historical subject, purposely—and bizarrely—out of scale with the rest of the room. The only completely contemporary elements might be the strictly functional lighting fixtures, or simple metal shelving units for books or for the display of collections of decorative objects (though not *too* decorative, as the very notion of decoration is kept out of the picture here).

The look of stripped-down classicism—despite the use of antique pieces, and despite the deadpan irony of those outsized tapestries—tends to be rather cool and remote. For some Italians, it comes uncomfortably close to a design style they wish to repudiate: that is, Rationalism, or so-called "Mussolini Modern." During the late 1920s and 1930s, this style—also characterized by a combination of modern design and severe, updated classicism—was selected by the fascist regime to embody its supposedly rational, progressive goals. After World War II, Italian architects and designers rejected this style in an effort to start out fresh. In the past decade, though,

with Neo-Rationalists such as Aldo Rossi achieving great prominence in the present-day pantheon of world architecture, some feel that "fascist" design is enjoying something of a comeback in Italy. Indeed, some of the sternly elegant furniture created during the fascist period—most notably, several designs by Giuseppe Terragni—are now available as reproductions, and several current designs, in their rustic yet severe simplicity, remind some people of the fascist 1930s.

Aldo Rossi himself has recently designed a lovely, by no means fascistic-looking collection of furniture that includes tables, chairs, an armoire, a chest of drawers, and a tall cabinet. These pieces have an air of almost child-like purity. It is not, however, so much the furniture as the chilly, monumental interiors and buildings that Rossi and his Neo-Rationalist colleagues create that alarm some Italian intellectuals. For them, harking back to a utopian Italian past with images of monolithic authority carries politically unsettling undertones. Yet the Neo-Rationalists themselves have stated on many occasions that their political sympathies do not lie with fascism, and that they have refined any lingering fascist traits out of their own work.

Neo-Rationalist architecture and interior design lack the kind of self-deflating humor that would assure its critics of its decent intentions. However, Rossi's furniture is certainly friendly looking enough. And though the stripped-down classical rooms do appear severe, there is often a humorous twist to them—the gigantic tapestry, say, or just one deliriously ornate baroque mirror over the fireplace—that lets people know that the mask of severity can be dropped at any moment.

As a matter of course, Italian homes, no matter in what part of the country they happen to be situated, are likely to boast an array of family heirlooms in the guise of furniture and furnishings, some centuries old. In some cases these objects might be casually set side by side with pieces of more recent vintage (think of those remote Tuscan farmhouses, furnished with old rustic pieces and, more recently, televisions!). In more formal rooms, those of the grand city palazzi and country villas, much of the original furniture might even still be employed; here, interiors will be not so much faithful reproductions of styles of the past as living examples of them. If a venerable old house has been restored, the owners might go to the trouble of furnishing its rooms with the same kind of objects that could

once have been there when the house was in its prime.

In the sumptuous homes of well-heeled Italian collectors, other approachs might be taken. Rather than maintaining the traditional pieces that originally filled a room, he or she will make a point of amassing designs from a favorite period of the past—rococo revival pieces of the late nineteenth century, for example; or pieces in the liberty style (that is, Italian art nouveau); or perhaps the Italian version of art deco that flourished in the twenties and thirties—and bring them together in such a way that they appear, not so much authentic, as a lush exaggeration of the epoch from which they hail. The typically Italian way of combining furniture, colors, textures, and proportions that characterizes even the most extreme contempo-

rary Italian interiors is brought into play here as well, even though the pieces might be antiques or, less frequently, reproductions.

Those antiques might be worth small fortunes—no matter. That sense of humor found so often in today's Italian interior design always makes its presence known, perhaps with a too-vivid marbleized finish on a room's moldings, or with a bit too much in the way of gilding, or with a large painting over the sofa whose subject matter is, depending on the period the collectors fancy, exaggerated.

Other Italian collectors may not favor any one period in particular, but rather find something to love in many. If his eye is especially keen, the collector will spot correspondences between furniture of the most diverse epochs and regions, and figure out ways to have them

Of Historic Interest

Right: Given the intense activity captured on this room's walls, simple, unobtrusive furniture was in order. The superb frescoes exemplify that in Italy, the past—at least in the decorative arts—is an ongoing, living tradition.

Though it is as sparsely furnished and architectural as any modern-style room, the one seen here has actually been restored and is several centuries old. It is a good example of how, in today's Italian interior design, past and present can come together seamlessly.

offset one another within a single room. He might not always choose a piece just because it is "tasteful." On the contrary, part of the humor in such an eclectic interior might come from the presence of some wonderfully cloddish-looking old relic, a little bit too vulgar for its own good, that would be included just for the fun of it.

This approach is not far removed from that which makes old English country homes so distinctive. The difference lies, again, in that characteristically Italian way of combining things, in which, even in an intentionally cluttered room, pieces stand out despite the play of pattern-against-pattern with architectonic clarity.

Other rooms might acquire a magical quality from murals that depict realistically rendered yet imaginary landscapes, and blur the distinction between indoors and out. Other murals might be less realistic, and rely for their effect on an unintentional crudity of execution—a crudity particularly strange when juxtaposed against the noble architectural detailing of some restored townhouse or villa.

The dream rooms exhibit a quality that can also be found in most intriguing Italian interiors today—a sense of drama. The drama is never forced. Often, as has been noted, there is at least some comic relief on hand. But the dramatic placing-just-so of this or that piece—a placing that shows how much the owner cares about, and admires the object—is what makes the room compelling. It is as if each object had been isolated slightly from its fellows, so as to preserve its special aura. And, too, it is as if all these objects were part of some stage set, the ideal backdrop against which to play out those amateur yet highly polished theatricals that constitute Italian social life.

Dream Rooms

Some of today's Italian interior design shows a marked tendency towards the outlandish and dream-like. These rooms, though no less bizarre than those created by Memphis and Studio Alchimia, usually lack the elaborate theoretic justifications in which both those groups excel. Often they are extremely idiosyncratic and different from one another, much in the way that dreams vary from person to person. This idiosyncracy is perhaps more related to the personal visions realized in the set design of both Italy's present-day *transavaguardio* and older, equally inventive stage designers like Ezio Frigerio, than to design per se. Here, as in those set designs, we see a blending of surrealistic and electronic imagery, and juxtapositions of seemingly unrelated objects and materials that are far more radical than those clever yet never too outrageous contrasts that characterize most conventional, contemporary Italian interiors.

Another possible influence on the designers of these uncanny interiors might be a particular way of showing products in the design magazines, in which the latest home furnishings are worked into highly atmospheric, dream-like still lifes. The still lifes may not give readers "ideas" as to what to do with these objects once they have acquired them for themselves; rather, they invest these often pricey objects with a mysterious, indefinable allure. Like these still lifes, the dream rooms appeal to one in an irrational way that, for some, can be hard to resist.

The furniture and furnishings in these dream rooms, whether for residential or commercial use, are perhaps their most familiar-looking aspect. It is the backgrounds against which these are set that can be so peculiar. In an extraordinary jewelry showroom in Milan, designed by the architect DePas D'Urbino Lomazzi, the walls slant at cockeyed angles and crack open crazily to reveal display cases filled with what looks like dazzling golden sand, worm-eaten red marble apples, gold bugs, and oxidized copper surfaces. Elsewhere in the showroom, a table-like structure draped with a rock-solid, blue marble-surfaced tablecloth (it was actually built up with plaster on a frame of wire) snakes here and there, in and out of doorways, past a stone sphere dropped at random on the floor, and fish-tank-like display cases with more golden sand in them. As is typical for such interiors, the lighting (including the ever-popular "Tizio" lamp, which is perhaps the epitome of the sleek, contemporary Italian style of design) and furniture (including a sofa from Memphis, which actually appears quite staid in these surroundings) are less outlandish.

Right: Trees and fountains seem to grow out of the walls of this fanciful interior. Needless to say, a room like this one would not be filled with furniture—the walls are the focus of visual interest.

Left: Piero Fornaseti created this *Citta di Carte/Bosco* printed, four-paneled screen in the early 1950s.

Chapter 2

Crafts

A tray cloth that combines various refined stitches—the shade stitch, the festoon stitch, and the simple grass stitch—makes an eye-catching centerpiece.

Cutlery and Tableware

In Italy, the human need to feed ourselves has always gone hand in hand with the aesthetic need to eat good food in a beautiful setting.

Since the Roman Empire, mealtime has meant more than mere satisfaction of a physical necessity. History details the well-turnished Roman tables, laden with extrava-gant displays of game, meat, fish, fruits, and vegetables from the far reaches of the empire. In ancient times, a table richly dressed with expensive cookware and delicate glass-work was considered a necessary status symbol for the upper classes. The way in which a society honors mealtime has come to be an important measure of civilization.

Italy has been profoundly divided throughout its eventful history. The language of a Venetian and a Sicilian is no more alike that that of a Spaniard and a German. Political, economic, social, and climatic differences have left the cultural life of the various regions of Italy with few points in common. But on one issue there is little argument: All Italians appreciate good food and the pleasure of eating at a beautifully decorated table with family and friends.

Italian tables are dressed with tablecloth and napkins two times a day: at noon and again at 8:00 P.M. Tablecloths, together with bed and bath linens, make up the trousseau of every Italian bride. Tablecloths differ in relation to the occasion for which they are to be used: white or colored cotton for everyday use; embroidered for Sundays, special

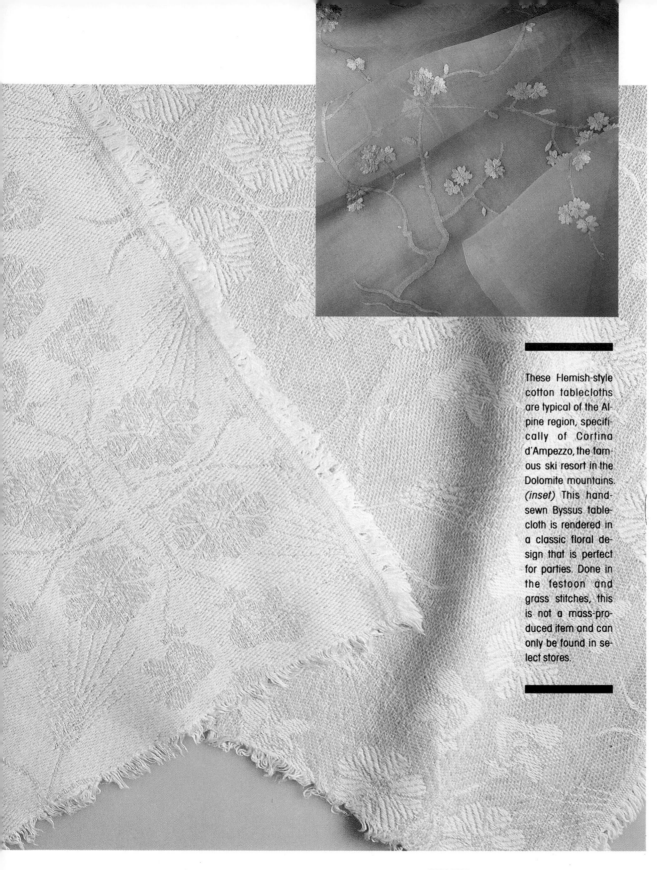

These Flemish-style cotton tablecloths are typical of the Alpine region, specifically of Cortina d'Ampezzo, the famous ski resort in the Dolomite mountains. *(inset)* This hand-sewn Byssus tablecloth is rendered in a classic floral design that is perfect for parties. Done in the festoon and grass stitches, this is not a mass-produced item and can only be found in select stores.

occasions, Christmas, and Easter. The handcrafting and use of fine tablecloths and napkins is so embedded in Italian culture that the handicraft prospers to this day in many Italian regions.

Every province in Italy has a characteristic, unique approach to tableware. Cortina D'Ampezzo, in the Dolomite Mountains, produces a beautiful local cloth similar to Flemish design, with both negative and positive patterns. The shops in the area supply tablecloths, centerpieces, and placemat sets of various sizes. If non-standard sizes are needed, a small factory in the town of San Candido, a few kilometers from Cortina, specializes in tablecloths made to order.

In Orta, a town in Piedmont, tablecloths are made with printed fabric. Great colorful geometric and floral designs derived from natural substances are stamped on huge lengths of raw linen. Yellows, for example, come from an ochre coloring extracted from the rust of iron. Arezzo, a town in the heart of Tuscany, uses an almost identical method of production, differing only in its more intricate design patterns.

Florence, among its many rich wares, offers embroidered tablecloths of the finest quality. For centuries nuns and orphans were commissioned to embroider the trousseaus of great Florentine ladies—layettes for their newborns, draperies, and bed linen. It is now possible to find not only the current, quality products, but also many antique items.

The islands also offer various surprises. Sardinia is especially known for its truly original fabric design. Sewn by hand in lively colors, Sardinian products are characterized by intricately costumed figures, found on everything from tablecloths to bedspreads,

A splendid, ornate design of the late baroque style, this antique silver set cannot be easily placed on a modern table as it would require china and a tablecloth of equal ornamentation. This table is arrayed with a salmon colored, cotton tablecloth embroidered by hand with floral design that resemble eighteenth-century patterns. The border of the cloth is finished with a delicate lace, hand-sewn with a soft Scottish thread.

shawls, and purses. Sicily is also active in this particular craft. Its most famous and valuable pattern is known as the *sfilati di Ragusa*, a loosely woven fabric often used for centerpieces.

On an international scale, Italian textile industries have always been noted for their ability to fuse the best of technology with all the detail of secular art. Here is a brief listing of the principal firms whose products may be found in elegant shops all over the world: Anele Zeta, Naj Oleari, T & J Vestor, and Bassetti. All produce printed cloths for tablecloths, bedspreads, and upholstery for sofas and chairs. Galimberti, Bossi, Telene, and Tessilarte also produce linen table-cloths of many shades with colored borders or scalloped edges. Partic-ularly Tessilarte, based in Florence, specializes in dyeing linen cloths to unusual shades of beautiful color. Frette, Borbonese, and Pratesi are considered the "greats" of the industry and are known all over the world. They produce beige, Flemish-style tablecloths, linens with lace appliques and embroi-dery in the finest Italian tradition.

For those who enjoy browsing for table linens and wares, we recom-mend a visit to the flea markets

scattered all over Italy (held in Milan the first Sunday of every month on the Naviglio canals; in Bollate, a few kilometers from Mi-lan, every Sunday; at Porta Portese in Rome, every Sunday; in the town of Sarzana, in the province of Massa Carrara, every September; and in every region at various times), where it is still possible to find some great buys. Often one can discover incomplete sets of *argento* (silver) or *argentone* (an impure silver alloy, also called "Broggi" after its manufacturer).

Indeed, silverware of all kinds is of great antiquarian interest. On via Montenapoleone in Milan, for example, a famous antiques shop displays a box containing six fruit knives with gold blades and carved handles, a masterpiece of the goldsmith trade.

Full silver services are also a part of Italian traditional handiwork. Silver companies are quite pro-ductive and their catalogues contain a rich variety of styles, from smooth, modern designs suitable for all tables, to more ornate, intri-cate shapes that reproduce an-tique designs.

Some of the more well-known silversmiths are located in Milan. The following is a brief sampling.

Ricci: one of the most famous silver shops in Milan, its catalogue con-tains silver designs dating back over thirty years, in addition to the very newest available designs. Ricci also specializes in silver holders for crystal and glassware. Ganci: Besides silverware, this shop also produces vases, boxes, plates, and tea and coffee services, all in silver. Boggiali: This shop offers antique silver frames and boxes. Pomellato: Primarily known as a jeweler, this shop also produces silverware. San Lorenzo: This shop sells silverware designed by some of the most important Italian de-signers, like one by Afra and Tobia Scarpa that is comprised of eighty-nine pieces in stainless steel with beautiful silver handles.

A word about Broggi, the long-standing manufacturer that cre-ated "Broggi," a less valuable alloy of silver, similar to silverplate. Their factory is located in Melegnano (in the province of Milan). Broggi products can also be found in all the best houseware stores through-out Italy.

Recognizing the importance of cost and practicality, top Italian designers are now designing ex-quisite flatware services in stainless steel.

Margaret Courtney-Clarke

Ceramics, Pottery, and Earthenware

We have already stressed the importance of the dining table in Italian culture, not only from a gastronomic point of view but also from an aesthetic one. Examples of this tradition exist throughout Italian history. The luxurious tables of the Renaissance, with their wealth of splendid detail, have been portrayed by the paintings and manuscripts of that era. One only has to remember the painting by Leonardo da Vinci that portrays Gian Galeazzo Sforza and Isabelle of Aragon on the occasion of their marriage in 1489, or that of Pope Alexander VI, a Borgia, in honor of the marriage of his beautiful

daughter Lucrezia to Alfonso, Duke of Este. These paintings show a sample table setting was composed of more than twenty-four sugar castles. A fountain stood in the center of the room, equipped with twelve spouts from which gushed forth twelve different wines. Clearly there was more than food, drink, tablecloths, and silverware on these royal tables to exhibit the wealth and greatness of the times. Ceramics also occupied a position of great prestige. Plates, huge fruit bowls, and platters of all shapes and sizes were great works of art in their own right, brought out for the admiration of guests. Their splen-

dor served to affirm the host's life of limitless opulence.

Ceramica, the Italian word for ceramics, implies five different types of materials that at different stages can be seen as derived one from another.

Terracotta, of porous consistency and without any glaze, is naturally colored and has many uses. The most popular are as vases and planters, because the porousness of the material allows the plant roots to breathe freely.

Majolica (also known as *faenza*) is of porous consistency but has a glass-like opaque glaze. Its name is derived from the island of Majorca and was incorporated into the Italian language by Dante in the twenty-eighth canto of the *Inferno*. This material was named after Majorca not because the island was a center of majolica production, but rather because at the time Majorca was an important nexus of northern Mediterranean trade.

Terraglia, earthenware, is a white ceramic of fine, resonant impasto, laced with a transparent glaze that renders an object non-porous. Although it is not possible to identify its exact birthdate, we know that terraglia is older than majolica and originated in northern Europe (France, Holland, and England).

Gres, a compact, colored ceramic, has a glaze that almost always consists of a saline coating.

Finally, *porcellana* (porcelain), is also of very solid consistency. Its texture is hard, translucent, and resonant. When it is without glaze, it is known as *bisquit*. Existing in China at the end of the T'ang dynasty (618 to 907 A.D.), porcelain was brought to Italy in 1245 by Marco Polo in the form of a small white vase, now part of the great treasures of St. Mark's in Venice. The word "porcellana" appeared for the first time in *Milione* (Marco Polo's personal diary) and it is believed that its name derives from the small seashells (used as money in the Far East) whose shape and color resemble that of a little pig (*porcellino*)—from which came *porcella* and then *porcellana*.

Because they were brought exclusively from China, porcelain objects were few and far between. Cherished like precious gems, they were the prized possessions of the royalty that could procure them.

There were many attempts to manufacture porcelain in Europe, a process found to be far more difficult than the production of terracotta, majolica, or stoneware. In Italy, a manufacturer in Florence achieved great success. Between 1545 and 1590, under the auspices of the bountiful Great Duke of Tuscany, Francesco de Medici, a limited but precious collection was produced (mostly destined for the tables of Tuscan nobles), still known today as the "Porcellana Medici."

Another major accomplishment in the development of ceramics also occurred in Florence. Luca Della Robbia, a well-known Florentine sculptor of the early fifteenth century, invented glazes for terracotta. It is said that Della Robbia, putting together information from merchants who had travelled all over the Orient, particularly in the great Byzantine ports of Istanbul, Crete, and Alexandria, produced the first terracotta glazes.

At the time of the Renaissance, the growth of ceramic production was clearly linked to the commercial prosperity of the region. This was not only a result of the work of the great merchants of the era, but it was also due to the extraordinary initiative of individual artisans seeking new images for their art. These artists were interested in employing new materials as well as new forms that could be artisti-

cally expressive and utilitarian at the same time.

This desire to explore, this intense activity among artisans, was to form the basis of the proliferation of ceramic manufacturing. In the following centuries, this activity would spread throughout the peninsula.

Centers of ceramic production are scattered all over the country, although certain differences exist among them. Some centers have emerged thanks to financial support from the upper classes, and from artists rich in imagination and inventiveness. Other manufacturers, however, never ventured beyond more modest production of household items, never aspiring to any kind of artistic level.

The success of ceramics in Italy was noteworthy and immediate. By the 1700s great collectors appeared, stimulating a lively, active market that still flourishes today. Indeed, among these ceramic works are certain masterpieces that can rival any Central European efforts. Doccia, Ginori (now Richard-Ginori), Capodimonte in Naples, and Vinovo in Piedmont, are the representative manufacturers in the artistic arena.

But collecting majolica and porcelain, however fascinating, is difficult and expensive. First of all, it is extremely rare to find pieces that are still intact after one or two centuries. Furthermore, it is quite difficult to correctly ascertain the origin of a given piece, an attributable date, artist, and region of manufacture. A point of interest: On the back of each piece an artist usually inscribed his name, the date, and the region in which he worked, with a series of symbols (markings) used for identification, just as stamps are used in silverware. Unfortunately, it is possible to come across a piece that is not worth its market price because the

This vibrantly patterned coffee cup is made of fine porcelain and is decorated in the deco style. It is part of a complete set signed "Porcellane Serra."

This fine white porcelain cup comes from a coffee service produced by Richard before its merger with Ginori. It is dated circa 1870.

markings are false. In other words, on a piece that may never have had any markings, a dealer can imprint false markings to increase its selling value. Only an experienced eye that has seen a great many pieces is in a position to really distinguish an authentic piece from one that has been falsified. It is risky to expect expert judgment from a person without this necessary preparation.

The business of collecting ceramics does not show any signs of weakening. it is aided by the consistent interest of museums all over the world in exhibiting these works of art. The permanent collections of many Italian museums are rich in interesting examples of this craft. The most important among them:
• in Faenza, the Museo Internazionale Delle Ceramiche (International Museum of Ceramics), is the most important center in Europe for Italian and foreign ceramics. Their collection includes valuable examples of the Renaissance and Faenze styles.
• in Florence, the Museo Delle Porcellane (Museum of Porcelain).
• in Genoa, the Museo Degli Ospedali Civili (Museum of Civil Hospitals) houses a rich collection of pharmaceutical vases.
• in Messina, the Museo Nazionale (National Museum) containing precious majolica from the Calabria, Puglia, and Abruzzo regions.
• in Milan, the Castello Sforzesco in the Sezione Ceramiche (Sforza Castle, Ceramics Section) contains pieces that date back to the fifteenth century.
• in Naples, there are three important museums: the Museo Principe Aragona Pignatelli Cortes, including porcelain from Venice, Doccia, and Capodimonte; the Museo Nazionale della Ceramica Duca Martina; and the Museo di Capodimonte, with over three thousand items of porcelain and majolica gathered from the estates of Neapolitan royal residences.
• in Pesaro, the Museo Delle

The porcelain of this unusual antique smoking set is decorated with grotesque figures engaged in the act of smoking. This Richard product dates from 1885. Note that the sizes of the holders are determined by their use for cigarettes or cigars. This rare work, maybe the only one of its kind, comes from a private collection in Palermo.

Ceramiche, where one can view spectacular examples of ceramics from Urbino.

• and in Turin, the Museo Civico, with a rich variety of porcelain and majolica.

The most famous ceramics producer is still Richard-Ginori, which offers the most complete and varied selection available today. Their merchandise includes sets of many styles and designs suitable for all fine tables—coffee and tea services, breakfast sets, and containers for all sorts of modern uses.

The headquarters of Richard-Ginori is in Milan, and the store has branches in Milan, Rome, Florence, and Naples.

Other companies are: Luciano Mancioli, found in Lucca, Rome, and in Naples; and Carini, which specializes in decorated porcelain, found in Milan, Venice, Rome, and in Naples. Carini also produces quality ceramics.

Great changes in the Italian social pattern have also been reflected in the use of pottery. Gone are the days of great kitchens with cooks, scullery-maids, and lace-aproned domestics. The lady of the house these days has had to find a different, more practical way of entertaining. To accommodate this change, the market is producing elegant crockery and dinnerware that can easily be used in cooking and then transported directly to the table, items of colorful design and shape that are consistently being improved.

Thus, the precious ceramics of the past are the prized possessions of collectors or remain in luxurious households that are in a position to entertain "like they did in the old days." They have been replaced by brightly colored coordinating sets of great variety that adorn the dining room and also enliven the kitchen.

An exquisite example of Neapolitan craft, this brightly colored porcelain statuette dates from the middle of the nineteenth century and is signed "Capodimonte." (Milan, Private Collection)

Murano Glass

On July 24, 1982, Venice inaugurated the largest, most important exhibit of glassware ever assembled, "A Thousand Years of the Art of Glass in Venice," in the Palazzo Ducale on Saint Mark's Square.

During the four-month run of the exhibit, thousands of people from all over the world viewed the most valuable treasures of this

bled the most important craftspeople of the island, thereby guaranteeing the continued quality of production.

At the same time this cooperative initiative was formed, a new Museo Del Vetro Contemporaneo (Museum of Contemporary Glasswork) was built and is run by both the Municipality of Venice and the

The Venetian isle of Murano is unequalled for its quality hand-blown glass products. Nowhere in the world is glass made so elegantly and with such skill.

thousand-year-old art form. Glassblowing originated in Venice in 982 A.D., on the island of Murano in the Venetian archipelago. It is not yet clear why the activity was concentrated in Murano; it is known that the glass corporations and schools emerged in 1000 A.D. The convergence of artisans and glass masters in Murano from all over Italy and abroad caused a variegated and rich level of production. This activity made an extremely important economic contribution to the Republic of Venice. It is no exaggeration to say that Murano was and still is one of the world's most important producers of fine glassware.

Glass production has not been limited to items of common or household use. One has only to look at the stained-glass windows of Saint Mark's to acknowledge the artistic efforts of Murano glassmakers to beautify their city with their craft. Yet the most important products have always been the pieces made to adorn beautiful homes.

To protect the old, glorious furnaces of Murano from the emergence|of factories, in 1981 a consortium was established under the trademark *Vetri Murano* (Murano Glass). This consortium assem-

The bottle on the left is for water; note that the stopper has a concave top to hold a piece of lemon. The piece on the right dates from 1950 and is a classic example of the Venetian multi-colored glass-blowing technique.

Office of the Assessor of Culture. Soon it will be possible to view an extensive variety of actual Murano glass and a wide spectrum of techniques currently in use— filagree, colored pastes, and others.

Besides contemporary glass objects, Venice also holds great offerings for those interested in older, antique glassware. In the

ufacturers, the same names as those found in the old Venetian registers, now produce works signed by famous designers and architects. Among the most important are Carlo Moretti, Venini, Barovier e Toso, Seguso, and Salvati & Co.

In addition to workshop visits, the interested can also make excellent

calli and campielli (the small squares and tiny alleys of the city) one can come across small, excellent shops where it is still possible to find a bargain. Real "buys" are difficult to find because most Venetian glass can be expensive, yet well worth the price and much in demand. A piece from 1930 or 1950 is already well known to collectors, and has historic value on the market. Today the most fashionable collectible items are small liqueur glasses, dated before the turn of the century. Until the 1900s, liqueur glasses were manufactured along with wine and water glasses. Nowadays, they are difficult to find.

Even for those who are only interested in antique glass, a visit to the furnaces of Murano is a definite must. Indeed, it has become a common practice of artisans, perhaps out of their own pride or their desire to attract tourists, to give demonstrations of the glassblowing process. The great masters are true artists who fiercely protect secrets passed down for hundreds of years. At scheduled times, they demonstrate their craft in laboratories situated inside beautiful, rustic courtyards.

Glass production has, of course, adapted itself to modern times. The names of the most important man-

These two handblown and delicately painted perfume bottles are wonderful examples of the many reasonably priced glass items available along the Veneto lagoon.

purchases. Sets of glasses, decanters for alcohol, water, and wine, and paperweights of all kinds (among them the famous Murrine, a glass ball filled with colored pieces forming geometric designs), are all available at reasonable prices. Knick-knacks, including the famous glass figurines of animals, clowns, flowers, and marionettes, are all available in the little stalls along the lagoon. And, of course, one can find exquisite antique collectible pieces at the shops mentioned above and at other outlets.

Commercial production in Venice also offers a wide variety of glassware applications, including lamps, stained glass for public buildings, and fixtures for big hotels and museums all over the world.

Lace

For centuries, handcrafted lace has been a part of every Italian bride's dowry in all social classes, in all regions. The Italian art of lace-making is one of the best examples of a traditional craft that has remained undisturbed by the consumer market. Passed down from mother to daughter, the craft of lace-making in Italy has held onto the same traditional techniques that were employed hundreds of years ago. Most lace production in Italy takes place in the home and is bound up in the everyday life of the community.

Types of lace are as varied as the uses for which they are intended: from elegant bridal veils to centerpieces on tables, from the ornate borders of bed linens to bedspreads, blankets, towels, and tablecloths. The fashion industry is often subject to rapid, inexplicable changes. For some time, lace was not a fashionable item. Now, however, lace appears not only on elegant bridal wear, but also on the evening dresses of Italy's great designers. Specialty stores such as Jesurum in Milan and Venice, which deal exclusively in lace and

This delicate, gossamer-like lace fan dates back to the end of the eighteenth century. A rare collector's item, it is in perfect condition and is signed "Jesorum Venice." Of particular interest is the mother-of-pearl handle.

embroidery, have swiftly regained popularity.

New stores have also sprung up. A store recently opened in Rome that is a veritable paradise of lacework. It is an antiques shop nestled in the old quarter of Trastevere. The owners, after searching the attics of Italy and Europe, have accumulated a fabulous collection of curtains, lingerie, tablecloths,

centerpieces, and even wedding dresses over one hundred years old. Their store champions the most famous lace patterns: *tombolo, chiacchierino, filet, macramé,* the Milan stitch, the Venice stitch, and all types of embroidery. Lace dating from the end of the eighteenth century can be very costly. Lace from the middle to the end of the nineteenth century is less expensive but by no means cheap.

The lacework of local craftspeople is found throughout Italy in the stalls in the city piazza or the shops of mountain towns, created by artisans who still practice age-old techniques.

Venice is one of the leaders in lace production, especially on Burano, an island easily reached by the famous *vaporetti*. Since 1100 A.D., the lace trade was centered in Burano, supported mostly by the wives of fishermen and farmers. Burano's Piazzetta de Portofino offers a variety of elegant shops and famous restaurants, and, on a typical summer afternoon, women can be found working in the celebrated chiacchierino pattern, a lace that is characteristic of Northern Italy. This delicate lace is the result of complicated intricate techniques and can be quite costly.

Lace is also found in the Alpine regions, where inhabitants have been forced to be self-sufficient. A traveller should not be surprised to find many Alpine areas producing their own laces and linens.

It is the region of Abruzzi, however, that is considered the real birthplace of lace production. For centuries in these rugged mountains, women have always worked in the *tombolo* (pillow-lace) pattern. It is a lace formed with *fuselli,* small wood sticks that weave the fine threads into finished lace. Two provinces in this region are specifically noteworthy: L'Aquila, where women work dressed in local black garments (probably of Oriental origin) and Lanciano, in the province of Pescara, where there is a school located in a medieval castle.

Florence, the cradle of Italian culture, is also known for this handiwork. Here, the production of lace, as with linens, stems from age-old tradition, tradition that is exemplified in the trousseaus of the most refined and wealthy Italian brides. In Florence, the making of lace and embroidery is not centered in the stalls of the squares. Rather it is produced by the nuns of the city's convents who have created lace that has made the *Punto Firenze,* or the "Florentine Stitch" so famous. Navone, on the left side of the Pont Vecchio, is the most popular store,

but many others are also found in the historic city center.

In the mountains of Pistoia, a region of Tuscany, the women of the tiny town of San Baronto are still commissioned for their work. Their craft is of the finest quality and consequently their prices tend to be quite high.

For the real devotees of fine lacework who wish to delve deeper into the history of the art, we recommend the Poldi Pezzoli Museum in Milan on via Morone. An entire section of the museum is devoted to Italian laces and embroidery.

Chapter 3

Cuisine

In keeping with a centuries' old tradition, some vineyards continue to age their wine in wooden casks.

One of the greatest treasures of Italy is the food. The preparation, presentation, and consumption of food is the cornerstone of Italian daily life. No one enjoys eating more than an Italian, and who can blame him. No other country in Europe offers such an infinite variety of gustatory experience, from the exquisite simplicity of Tuscan food to the spicy Oriental flavors of Sicilian fare. Many non-Italians still believe that Italian food consists of little more than spaghetti and pizza. Nothing could be further from the truth. There is no such thing as a homogeneous Italian cuisine. There are as many approaches to cooking in Italy as there are provinces and regions. It must be remembered that, up until the nineteenth century, Italy was a country divided into many separate states, each with its own fiercely guarded and zealously maintained gastronomic traditions. Also, these regions had different climates and geography, which allowed for a wide range of agriculture, meat, dairy, and fish products, further adding to the enormous diversity of this country's cuisine. The same can be said of different towns belonging to a single region, such as Catania and Palermo in Sicily, or Venice and Treviso in Veneto.

When Caterina de Medici became the bride of Henri II, the Dauphin and soon-to-be King of France, she brought along as part of her dowry a half-dozen Italian cooks to civilize the barbaric sixteenth century French cuisine. Caterina made a point of including in her royal gastronomic team only Florentine chefs, rejecting those of Siena and Arezzo because of "their lack of refined expertise and rich imagination." The two cities, a few dozen miles from Florence, paid back this derogatory and unwarranted remark by naming a variety of pork dishes after her, such as *Porchetta Caterina* or *Caterinetta a lo spiedo*. Even today, Sienese and Aretino cooking is clearly distinguishable from Florentine cooking.

Differences rooted in such a fractured historical tradition are compounded by climatic conditions which vary considerably from north to south. Italy, *"das Land wo die Citronen blühn,"* is a sunny country all right, but raspberries are picked in the snowclad forests of the Alps, while prickly pears

grow wild in Sicily; less than forty miles separate the giant palm trees of Piazza di Spagna in Rome from the birch trees and the apple orchards of the Appenine hills.

Regional cuisines inevitably reflect the diversity of climates which determines local produce through the changing seasons. That is why the best approach to a gastronomical tour of any town is a visit to its vegetable, fish, and meat markets, some of them historical landmarks like Piazza delle Erbe in Verona or Campo de'Fiori in Rome. The displays are master-pieces in themselves, executed in the grand manner of the Renais-sance painter Carlo Crivelli: fes-toons of tangerines intermingled with lemons and green leaves, artichokes arranged in triumphal heaps, hams, fowl, and strings of sausages—fresh, or dry in the Sien-ese fashion—cascading from horizontal poles, cheeses framed by ferns and laurel, and the end-less cornucopia of lush fruit and vegetables, presented in a chro-matic scale encompassing the red of Treviso's *radicchio,* the dark green of zucchini, the purple-black of eggplant, the velvety yellow of peaches, and the full rainbow of lettuces. The scenario belongs to the commedia dell'arte: vendors soliciting buyers with bombastic exaltations of their products, hu-morous haggling over prices, and the recurring innuendoes about the conjugal misfortunes of whom-ever at the moment is the Minister of Taxation. Bakeries *(panifici)* and pastry shops *(pasticcerie)* are clustered around the open-air markets, feasts for the eye and nose. Oven-fresh and gold-crusted, the Roman *rosetta,* a round and hollow bread, keeps company with the nationally produced *sfi-latino,* a shorter version of the French *baguette.* Side-by-side rest four or five varieties of *casareccio,*

The preparation of spinach gnocchi re-quires the work of skilled hands.

Margaret Courtney-Clarke

Every town in Italy has a specialty store called *salumeria* where a variety of cured hams, smoked bacons, and sausages as well as cheeses are sold.

Margaret Courtney-Clarke

Olive vendors are a familiar sight in southern Italy where olives are a basic staple, particularly in Sicilian cooking.

large rustic loaves with or without salt, the *manina ferrarese,* a four-fingered and crisp hand, the *grissini,* breadsticks of various thicknesses and lengths, the *pizza bianca,* flat and shiny with olive oil and salt, and its Bolognese relative, the *piadina.* Bakeries usually include a pastry section, but pastry shops do not sell bread. Amongst the variety of cakes, *torte* is determined by regional origin or relates to the season and a particular festivity. *Pasta reale,* an almond paste stuffed with candied citron, is a Sicilian specialty, shaped like a baby lamb and eaten at Easter time. In Northern Italy the same religious occasion is celebrated with the *colomba,* a sweet bread cake in the shape of a dove stuffed with almonds, and very similar in texture to the taller *panettone,* the pride of Milan at Christmas time. Venetian pastry is influenced by the Viennese and Hungarian masters, while *cenci,* elsewhere called *frappe*—stripes of fried dough covered in powdered sugar—is a Florentine invention. Nowadays it can be found all over the peninsula. The Bolognese *zuppa Inglese* and the *Mont Blanc,* richer—if that's possible—variations of *blanc mange* and *trifle,* present an irresistible challenge to any calorie-conscious epicure. The same is true of the small Italian pastries *bignes,* cream or chocolate-filled puffs, *diplomatici,* rectangular layers of flaky pastry, custard, and whipped cream, and the tiny multicolored fruit pies with a thousand different names.

Shopping for pastry on Sunday morning is a ritual of the Italian male, as strictly observed as the daily shopping by women in the open-air marketplaces. It may have something to do with guilt and the cleansing of "conjugal sins," but around noon on the day of the Lord, a multitude of contrite men can be seen tiptoeing out of the *pasticcerie* with their shiny paper-wrapped *pastarelle,* on their way home to celebrate a tradition of familial bliss, the Sunday lunch.

The importance and sacredness of wine as an economic activity and social ritual throughout Italian history is a tradition joyfully kept alive by all Italians. The social element surrounding the drinking of wine as an accompaniment to good food is a tradition upheld in the home, at *trattorie,* restaurants, and in inns, or *osterie.* The latter were once considered places of ill repute, where peasants, transformed into industrial workers by the advent of industrialization, would go on payday for easy and ruinous consolation. But today *l'osteria,* together with the bar, is an innocent meeting place for people who wish to exchange pleasantries while imbibing a glass of fine wine or the numerous types of aperitifs, such as *campari,* vermouth, or sherry. More recently, *prosecco,* a dry white bubbly wine, has come into vogue as yet another aperitif.

Each region of Italy produces its own characteristic wines, grown from vineyards strictly controlled by consortiums which guarantee their purity and regional integrity. However, for the less demanding wine-lover the local wines offered in carafes by restaurants are also of excellent quality.

In conclusion, a stranger to Italian regional cuisine should keep an open mind and not shy away from what may seem like exotic dishes. The ancient gastronomic traditions, combined with regional and seasonal trends, and distinct shopping habits dictated by the pursuit of the freshest produce, make this cuisine one of the most varied and exciting in Europe.
Buon Appetito!

These two northernmost regions of Italy are generally considered to have the richest and most diverse gastronomic traditions. The geography of this region varies from the fertile plains of the Po River to the imperious Alpine frontier. Piedmont's history, dialect, and way of life are very similar to that of the nearer parts of France. Piedmont produces more than sixty percent of the nation's rice and is one of the largest breeders of cattle and producers of dairy products in all of Italy. Lombardy is also one of the most populous and productive regions of Italy, comprising almost a fifth of the national population, and is responsible for an equally large share of the nation's GNP, half of which consists of agricultural and livestock production. The basic culinary elements of both regions are rice, butter, garlic, milk, and cheese. Among the regional

A Gastronomic Tour of Italy from North to South

Piedmont and Lombardy

Many Italian restaurants display their mouthwatering specialties in sidewalk windows to lure customers inside.

Grilled and dressed with olive oil, garlic, and parsley, these mushrooms make an unforgettable dish.

delicacies, one must taste the array of seasonal mushrooms, from the delicious and internationally renowned *porcini* (boletus), to the more common *gallinacci* (chanterelles), and *ovoli* (agaric). With the opening of the hunting season, mouthwatering additions to restaurant menus consist of *pernici* (partridges), *faggiani* (pheasant), *anitre* (ducks), and *lepre* (hare). Throughout the year the crown jewel of both regions is the prized *tartufo*, truffle, an expensive, pungent delicacy worthy of its reputation and used as a condiment in almost every dish.

A typical meal should start with any of a number of exquisite antipasti. Purposefully prepared to entice one's appetite, they cover a wide gamut of ingredients produced locally. Antipasti range from *carpaccio* or *tagliata,* thin slices of raw fillet of beef dressed with lemon, topped with shavings of parmesan and white truffles to an assortment of local sausages, prosciuttos or *crostini,* thin slices of toasted bread covered with a light sauce of oil, butter, anchovies, garlic, and parsley. A typical first course is the classic *risotto,* a rice dish prepared with chopped onions sautéed in butter, into which the rice is added and cooked while slowly adding a meat-based broth and other diverse ingredients. When in Milan, the *risotto alla Milanese* is a must, characterized by the addition of pure saffron just a few minutes before serving in order to preserve its delicate aroma. Try any of the many meat and pork dishes as a second course—their exquisiteness reflects the long tradition and great quantity of these regions' livestock production. *Costoletta alla Milanese,* a veal cutlet dipped in beaten eggs, covered with bread crumbs, and fried in butter is a typical second course, usually served with a side dish, or *contorno* (which literally means *surrounding*), of asparagus, roasted mushrooms, or string beans. A Turinese dish that must be tried is the *bagna cauda,* a type of fondue based on a pungent mixture of oil, garlic, and anchovy, into which one dips various vegetables such as edible thistle, peppers, or celery. Usually this dish is accompanied by a robust red wine, either the intense, velvety, and dry *Barolo,* or the characteristic and austere *Barbaresco.*

The varied agricultural production is also reflected in a wide assortment of delicious fruits, from pears and apples to apricots, peaches, strawberries, raspberries, and cherries.

Finally, almost all of Italy's cheeses are produced in both regions. The more typical include an intense variation of parmesan cheese called *bagoss,* or the milder, softer, and fruitier *taleggio,* or the sweet and buttery *bel paese.*

For those not used to consuming abundant meals, eating in Piedmont or Lombardy is always a serious and involved affair. One suggestion is to control the enthusiasm provoked by the varied and delicious antipasti (a restaurant patron can be presented with an assortment of up to thirty!). The predominant wines found in these two regions are produced in Piedmont. In addition to the red wines mentioned are the *Barbera d'Alba,* with a dry, slightly tannic, full-bodied taste, or the dry, austere *Barolo.* All are to be tasted with meats or game.

Today most wine growers have replaced the wooden poles of their vineyards with cement ones. This vineyard remains an exception.

Margaret Courtney-Clarke

Liguria

The capital of this coastal region
is Genoa, one of the great seafaring republics of Italy during the
Renaissance and today a center of
shipping. With a modest agricultural production, its moderate
marine climate encourages the
growth of a wide variety of wild
and cultivated aromatic herbs
such as basil, rosemary, thyme,
sage, and lavender. The cooking of
this region is characterized by its
simplicity and the lack of animal
fats in the preparation of many of
its dishes. The gastronomy of Liguria is governed by the exception-
ally subtle aroma of herbs such as
basil and marjoram. Although its
coastal geography would suggest
a rich variety of fish dishes, this is
not so, due to the relative scarcity
of fish in the Ligurian Sea. One of
the few authentic fish specialties is
the *Cappon Magro*, (a rich and
laboriously prepared Genoese fish
salad). Six or seven types of fish are
cooked separately with seasoned
vegetables and placed in layers
on a base of sea biscuits soaked in

vinegar. The numerous layers form a pyramid, which is covered with a rich sauce concocted largely of oil and anchovies. This elaborate preparation is then presented on a spectacular plate decorated with slices of hard-boiled egg, lobster medallions, oysters, giant shrimp, and other crustaceans. A good, dry, and pleasantly fresh local white wine to complement this dish is the *Pigato di Albenga.* However, one can choose from a wide variety of white and red wines traditionally imported from other regions, especially Tuscany and Piedmont.

The queen of Ligurian sauces is the *pesto,* a raw, ground mixture of the purest virgin olive oil, delicate Genoese basil, pinoli nuts, garlic, and parmesan cheese. Also characteristic of this cuisine are the variety of stuffed vegetables—zucchini or courgettes, onions, eggplant or aubergines, tomatoes, and peppers—which are roasted and stuffed with their own pulp mixed with bread crumbs, spices, and occasional additions of chopped prosciutto, eggs, or cheese. Unlike the Venetians, Ligurians have never accepted exotic spices in their cuisine. However, they did learn to prepare candied fruits and use them in a variety of cakes and pastries. Their version of the Milanese Christmas specialty *panettone* is a light sponge cake prepared with an assortment of candied fruits and particularly rich in raisins, pinoli nuts, and citron. The Ligurian version is called *pandolce.* Middle Eastern imports to Liguria are salted or sweet flat breads such as the *focaccia,* sprinkled with oil and salt and cooked in an oven until golden and crisp.

Unlike the case in any other Italian region, it is difficult to make a clear distinction between antipasti and first courses. Almost all

the abundant stuffed vegetable preparations and different salted cakes are presented as an assortment of tastes, or *assaggi,* to inspire the appetite. Together with these antipasti are those acquired from the cuisines of surrounding regions, such as various types of *carpacci* or *tagliate.*

As a first course one should taste the native *pesto* sauce served with a commercially produced pasta called *trenette,* (a smaller version of the northern *tagliatelle,* prepared without eggs). The second course could consist of *Coniglio in umido,* succulent pieces of rabbit fried in oil and butter, garlic, rosemary, onions, and white wine, with a sprinkle of black olives and pinoli. Another suggestion for a second course is the *Vitello all'uccelletto,* pieces of veal cooked with oil, butter, laurel, white wine, and, when in season, artichoke hearts.

Margaret Courtney-Clarke

Known as *argentelli,* or whitebait, these baby fish are delicious when fried with a drop of fresh lemon; this delicacy provides the basis for a tasty meal by the sea.

Strings of onion and small red hot peppers called *peperoncini* are a staple in any self-respecting Italian kitchen.

Radicchio, a red leafed bitter lettuce, is indigenous to northern Italy where it is either grilled or served fresh with slices of orange.

A Venetian shop-keeper in front of a gastronomic mural.

Margaret Courtney-Clarke

Venetia

The topography of this region, which faces the Adriatic Sea, includes lagoons, plains, hills, and mountains, reflecting an equally varied agricultural and livestock production. Unlike the other seafaring republic of Genoa, the city of Venice offers a rich tradition of marine products, including the cultivation of crustaceans and molluscs of excellent quality. The mixture of varied agricultural production and rich fishing industry provides Venetia with the privilege of having one of the most complete and refined cuisines. Two essential features distinguish this cuisine from the rest: The first is the constant presence of cornmeal, out of which *polenta* is made (by boiling cornmeal in water until it thickens). It is eaten plain, used as a base for various sauces, or cut into slices for frying, baking, or grilling. The other feature is the frequent use of ingredients originating in the Orient (such as an assortment of spices and Corinthian raisins), which reflect the great Venetian sea trading tradition. Together with *polenta,* rice is also a staple and is prepared in so

Freshly cut parsley and rosemary on display in a vegetable store.

many different ways that the variety seems limited only by the local market's produce or the imagination of feisty Venetian cooks. *Risotti* are made with sausages, tripe, milk, and sultana raisins, celery and tomato, pumpkins, pigskin, chicken livers or beans, quail; with sauces deriving from all kinds of fish or vegetables, from asparagus tips to lettuce and the Venetian *radicchio.* As for fish, in addition to the fish caught in the Adriatic, one must mention those of the surrounding lakes and lagoons which provide the local cuisine with a wide variety of fresh and saltwater fish, including sea bass (*branzino*), mullet (*muggine*), gilt-head (*orata*), sole (*sogliola*), eel (*anguilla*), and a number of edible crustaceans, from snails (*lumachine*) to oysters

(*ostriche*), mussels (*cozze*), and soft shell crabs (*moleche*). When using meat, Venetian cooking concentrates on small animals and white meats such as lamb, young goat, chicken, or capon. Other characteristic meats are those of the guinea-fowl and duck. Of the game dishes the most interesting is *Polenta e osei,* made with small birds (*osei* in the Venetian dialect), and presented on a bed of *polenta.* In addition to various national cheeses, there are several typical of the region, such as *asiago,* a firm yellow cheese with small, evenly scattered holes and a hard, golden rind, and *montasio,* similar in taste to *asiago,* but springy when young and hard and brittle after a year or two of aging.

Start a meal with the antipasto

Baccala' mantecato, dried cod steamed with salt, pepper, nutmeg, and chopped parsley, beaten with a wooden spatula, and mixed with olive oil until it reaches the consistency of mayonnaise. It is then briefly sautéed and served. While in the city of Venice one must try as a first course, the sublime *Risotto alle Seppie,* a rich dish made of cuttlefish and its ink, which gives a black tint to the rice. As a second course, any of a wide variety of *orata,* gilt-head, or deep water fish are excellent. A characteristic second course on the island of Murano is the *bisato sull'Ara.* Exquisite in its simplicity, it is made of eel cooked in a saucepan with laurel. Most of the eel fat melts and the result is a delicious, lean dish. In addition to the traditional Venetian

biscuits, the so-called *caramei* or *golossesi* are interesting and fun. Nuts, dried figs, and prunes or apricots are skewered on a stick, immersed in caramelled sugar, and presented in a colorful array in the shape of a fan.

It has been written that good Venetian wine has comforted the Venetians for over a thousand years, sparking their imaginations and strengthening their bodies. Tasting the local wines is a delightful confirmation of these legends. A savory white wine, ideal with crustaceans and fish soups, is the *Bianco di Custoza.* It is lightly aromatic, soft, and delicate in taste, while the dry and slightly tart *Bardolino* is an excellent accompaniment to soups, white meats, and light game.

It takes six to twelve months to cure Italy's world renown prosciutto.

A colorful tray of *bussetto,* a pasta specialty of the Emilia-Romagna region.

Emilia-Romagna

Margaret Courtney-Clarke

This entire region is characterized by a large agricultural output due to its wide and fertile plains and strong tradition of market garden produce. With this tradition in mind, one can understand how this abundant and generous cuisine developed over the centuries by catering to the labor-intensive needs of its inhabitants. Today, though these needs have been greatly reduced by modernization and the development of other manufacturing industries, the Emiliani and Romagnoli have jealously maintained their cuisine's distinct richness. A gastronomic trek through this region offers an incredible amount of exciting eating opportunities.

The production of pork products holds an important place in Emilia-Romagna as in no other Italian region. The manufacturing concerns surrounding the province of Parma receive more than a million pork haunches a year, and transform them into prosciutti sold throughout the world. As a whole, the cuisine of this region is based on pork products and a variety of first courses in which *tortellini* predominates (a small pasta shaped like an ear and stuffed with a mixture of ham, mortadella, sausage, chopped chicken, pork or veal, eggs, nutmeg, and parmesan, usually served in stock with cream or tomato sauce). Other notable agricultural products include potatoes, plentifully cultivated around Bologna; cardoons or *cardi;* artichokes from Cesena; and a small, rather flat sweet onion grown around Parma named *cipolle parmigiane.* This region also grows exquisite fruit and the best cherries in all of Europe. The coastal areas encompassing the centers of Rimini and Cesenatico are renowned for the freshness of their fish. In addition to a series of sea antipasti, a locally produced broth consisting of red mullet (triglie), brill (rombo), scorpion fish (cappone), sole, and others is typical of the region. The variety of fish is also evident in the famous misti griglia, or mixed grills.

Finally, the most important ingredient in the gastronomic repertoire of this fertile region is parmesan cheese, or grana. Produced in the region of Parma, Reggio Emilia, Modena, and Bologna, the only cheese that can claim the stamp of the Parmiggiano Reggiano consortium delights the palate with a nutty, buttery flavor that makes it one of the most celebrated cheeses in the world. Parmesan has to be made with the milk of animals freely grazing in country pastures. Strictly regulated by the consortium bearing its name, this cheese must be made between the first of April and the eleventh of November. It has been praised by name for at least two hundred years (Molière is said to have lived largely on parmesan during his declining years), but the grana family of cheeses was being made in Italy even before the advent of the Romans. In addition to parmesan, the region produces excellent butter and fresh or seasoned pecorino cheese, literally meaning small sheep. Made from ewe's milk, pecorino is decidedly piquant in flavor. The farther south in Italy one goes, the more sharp (piccante) the cheese becomes.

Unlike any of the other capitals of the regions we have covered, Bologna offers the visitor solely its own cuisine. In fact it is almost impossible to find dishes from other areas offered in Bolognese restaurants. This is understandable when considering the extraordinary cuisine of this province. Many travelers and Italians themselves will swear that the best food in Italy can be found in Bologna. There is even a copyrighted recipe named after the city: Ragū alla Bolognese, a sauce made with butter, prosciutto, a few onions, carrots, tomatoes, grated lemon peel, nutmeg, and, toward the end of its preparation, a spoon of cream to tie the ingredients together.

As an antipasto, a taste of the various prosciutti, sausages, and other pork products is suggested. A first course must include any of the different forms of stuffed pasta that this city is famous for, such as the Tortellini alla Bolognese. As a second course, Costoletta alla Bolognese is one of the most celebrated local dishes. It is made of breaded veal cutlets sautéed in butter, then placed in an oven after each cutlet has been covered with a slice of prosciutto, a thin slice of tender cheese (usually fresh parmesan), and finally laced with a tomato or meat sauce. For dessert one must try the Bolognese delicacy, Pan speziale, made with flour, honey, almonds, hazelnuts, sultanas, chocolate, pinoli, and assorted candied fruits, and flavored with clove, coriander, and cinnamon.

Due to a terrain ideal for grape growing, Emilia–Romagna produces some of the best table wines of Italy. The most famous red wines include the family of Lambrusco, sparkling, dry, and delicious with some of the more characteristic and heavy Bolognese dishes, and the San Giovese di Romagna, a dry and harmonious wine which leaves a pleasantly tart aftertaste and is excellent with the regional pasta dishes, meats, cheeses, and sausages. The perfect white wine to have with fish and antipasto is the dry and savory Trebbiano di Romagna.

Wheels of Parmigiano Reggiano, or grana, Italy's most famous cheese, need two to four years to develop their sharp and salty taste.

Margaret Courtney-Clarke

Margaret Courtney-Clarke

At the Villa Banfi the typical wooden support poles for the grape vines have been replaced with more weather resistant cement ones.

Tuscany

Hilly and mountainous, Tuscany has maintained, almost intact, an archaic peasant tradition tied to agricultural methods little affected by modern agricultural techniques. A recent census found that there are 125,000 agricultural laborers (out of a population of 3.5 million) working in 126,540 agricultural concerns, little more than one laborer per concern. This is one of the main reasons why Tuscan cuisine has managed to remain uncorrupted, continuing a gastronomic tradition based on simplicity and a fundamental respect for natural flavors and quality ingredients. Devoid of complicated sauces and gravies and elaborate preparations, Tuscan culinary triumphs consist of grilled, skewered, and fried meats and fish. The only ingredients used to enhance flavor are the aromatic herbs that are either cultivated or grown in the wild. Throughout the Tuscan countryside the traveler is bound to notice a multitude of wild rosemary bushes and can taste this distinct flavor in almost every dish, even in the traditional *castagnaccio* (chestnut) cake.

A fundamental ingredient in almost all the dishes of this region is extra-virgin olive oil. Controlled by a consortium that imposes rigid regulations concerning its production, it is produced in great quantities and renowned for its perfection and distinct, fruity flavor. Unlike other regions with similar peasant traditions, where white meats such as poultry and rabbits prevail, the leading meat of Tuscany is the succulent and seductive steak prepared in the Florentine manner, *bistecca alla Fiorentina*. Simply prepared, all one needs to fully enjoy this dish is a crisp *insalata mista* (mixed salad) and *patate fritte* (fried potatoes). The less important white meats are usually grilled or skewered.

Tuscan prosciutti are superb—smaller and leaner than those of Emilia–Romagna, yet cut into thicker slices when served as an antipasto or a snack. Moving toward the southernmost area of the region, Maremma, one can find exquisite prosciutti and sausages made from the wild boar that roam freely throughout the hilly, sun-

baked landscape. Vegetables also represent a very important contribution to this cuisine. Some are typical of the region, such as black cabbage used in unforgettable soups, or small white *cannellini* beans boiled with rosemary and doused with a drop of oil when served with freshly chopped tomatoes and basil. Throughout Italy, beans represent the humble ambassadors of Tuscany. It is from this region that their use in different dishes spread to the rest of Italy.

Notwithstanding the large cattle breeding in the Maremma and Chianina areas, Tuscany excels in the processing of sheep milk. Almost every county produces its own distinctive pecorino, the most famous one produced in and around Siena. Ricotta, a common soft cheese with a fine granular consistency, is also produced throughout the region, and is used as a filling for ravioli, cannelloni, or eaten fresh in different preparations, one of which is typically Tuscan: *Ricotta ubriaca,* or drunken (or inebriated) ricotta, because it is laced with brandy or rum.

An appropriate beginning to any meal in Tuscany is an order of *Crostini alla Toscana,* pieces of toasted casareccio bread generously spread with a mixture of veal spleen, and chicken livers or kidneys, layered in a pan with onions, anchovies, capers, and pepper. The sauce can vary according to the specialties of each town, village, or valley. Another essential antipasto or snack is the thickly sliced, lean Tuscan prosciutto of pork or wild boar *(cinghiale),* to-

gether with a variety of other sausages such as the characteristic *finocchiona,* a soft mixture of finely minced lean meats flavored with fennel seeds. A typical first course is the *acquacotta,* or cooked water, an ancient peasant dish valued even today as a local specialty. It is a thin soup made with onion, celery, and tomatoes lightly sautéed in olive oil and water. The whole concoction is seasoned with salt, small hot peppers, and toasted slices of casareccio bread immersed into the soup. Richer versions of *acquacotta* include beaten eggs and cheese. As a second course, *bistecca alla Fiorentina* should be tasted. It is a sirloin steak cooked on a grill without any condiments except for the salt, pepper, or lemon you add yourself. Another traditional sec-

ond course is the *Fritto misto,* or fried mix of croquettes of poultry, potatoes, calf brains, sweetbread, artichokes, pieces of liver and other scrumptious meats. Each ingredient is covered in flour, then dipped in beaten eggs and fried in olive oil. A fundamental secret of this preparation is the changing of the oil at every frying, a respected practice in the traditional restaurants that refuse to use the big automatic fryers. A final closing to these exquisite Tuscan meals are desserts such as the *biscottini di Prato,* small hard biscuits made with flour, egg whites, almonds, and pinoli and served with the delicious *Vin Santo,* a strong, lusciously sweet "holy wine." It is common to dunk the *biscottini* in the wine before popping them in your mouth, a custom that can be addictive! Another dessert typical of Siena is the *panforte* or "strong bread," a hard, thin cake made with flour, sugar, almonds, many candied fruits, and spices.

Volumes could be written on the famous wines of Tuscany, exported and consumed all over Italy. Who has not heard of Chianti? In addition to the bottled wines that can vary in quality from delicious to exceptional, are the numerous local wines, served in carafes and highly representative of the local taste and culture. One can never be disappointed by the dry *Chianti Classico* wines. One of the greatest wines of Italy produced in Tuscany is the precious *Brunello di Monalcino,* perfect with roasted meats and game. Tuscany is also a great producer of white wines that are excellent with fish dishes of all sorts. *Vernaccia di San Gimignano* is one of these, fresh and dry with a delicate and penetrating perfume. The soft and dry *Bianco di Pittigliano* is another great white wine and an appropriate accompaniment to any meal.

Fresh *maccheroni,* made with eggs and flour, are ready to be cooked.

Margaret Courtney-Clarke

At Christmas time Piazza Navona fills with candy stands where a variety of delicious sweets are made on the spot and sold by weight, to the delight of children.

Margaret Courtney-Clarke

Latium

Three of the five million inhabitants of this region live in Rome, and thus the cuisine throughout the region is characterized as "Roman." Its gastronomic traditions stem from the simple and elementary methods developed by the eating habits of shepherds and farmers. It is these characteristics that make Roman cuisine so attractive to the palate. To eat well in Rome means eating in an indulgent manner. The imagination is stimulated not so much by the notable quality of the food as by the loud and colorful choreography of the food presentation. Dominating the cuisine of this region is the *abbacchio al forno,* young milk lamb roasted in an oven, which can be found daily in every restaurant along with other lamb dishes prepared in different ways. The vegetables served also reflect Roman peasant traditions. The most famous of all Roman vegetables is the artichoke. It is a unique artichoke—round, free of spines at its center, and cooked *alla giuda* according to an old recipe that has rendered famous the restaurants of the Roman ghetto. In every marketplace of the capital, numerous national cheeses abound. An enormous variety of Roman pecorinos are brought to the city from the surrounding countryside, in addition to singular ricotta cheeses. One must not forget the variety of sea products introduced to the city from the ports of Civitavecchia and Fiumicino, including red mullet, fresh cod, simple mullet, Mediterranean bass (tastier and smaller than the Atlantic striped bass), sole, giant shrimp, and the typically Roman *mazzancolle,* a very large shrimp which is usually grilled.

A classic Roman meal must start with an antipasto of tangy, mouthwatering *bruschetta,* for which simple slices of casareccio, dipped in olive oil and rubbed with garlic, are then toasted in an oven or on a grill. A second course is another local specialty traditionally served on Thursdays (you can ask, but no Roman can agree on "why on Thursday?"), *Gnocchi alla Romana.* These are small dumplings made with potatoes and flour and served with tomato sauce, basil, and cheese. Another, less filling course is the hearty *Fettuccine all'amatriciana,* long flat strips of pasta made with eggs (usually called *tagliatelle* in Florence and the north), served with a sauce of bacon, tomatoes, onions, chili pepper, a drop of white wine, and finished with a generous dose of aged pecorino cheese. As an accompaniment to fried dishes or mixed cuts of meat *Carciofini sott'olio* are appropriate. *Carciofi alla Giuda* is an exquisite second course in which artichokes are cooked in oil and fried. This process keeps the artichokes from closing so that they may be presented open like flowers. Another classic second course is the *abbacchio alla cacciatora,* baby lamb either roasted, or as this recipe requires, prepared *in bianco* with garlic, rosemary, white wine, anchovies, and chili pepper. An excellent and appropriate dessert is the irresistible *crostata di ricotta,* a velvety cheesecake made with egg, Marsala, lemon, and a ricotta cheese filling.

Rich in an ancient tradition, the viticulture of Latium dates back to the time of Caesar. Pliny, Horace, Catullus, and other great poets have sung praises to the wines of Latium and Campania. Excellent table wines are produced in this region. Of the bottled variety the most prestigious is the dry white wine of Frascati, a perfect complement to any Roman dish.

The restaurant Otello alla Concordia in Via Condotti, Rome, is world renowned for its display of fruits and vegetables cascading over an ancient fountain.

Margaret Courtney-Clarke

A fish vendor readies her wares for market.

Campania

The terrain of this region is composed of fertile volcanic plains, valleys, and mountains. Coupled with an agreeable and constant climate, these conditions make possible a rich production of agricultural products. The basis of almost all Neapolitan cooking is the tomato and its diverse products, from sauces and preserves to salads. The best tomatoes in this region come from Salerno, San Mazano, and Torre del Greco. Campania is also known for its cauliflowers, peppers, artichokes, peas, beans, and the delicate and esteemed sweet onions from Avella. Small family orchards produce more than 150,000 tons of

The luscious bounty of Campania's rich volcanic soil.

Nuts and dried figs are often served with fresh fruit at the end of a meal or as an afternoon snack.

noteworthy fruits and vegetables each year. Less varied is the livestock production, although eighty percent of the nation's buffalo are found here, in addition to approximately 300,000 cows. The cheese of Campania are famous, beginning with the best *mozzarella,* fresh, rubbery, white cheeses made from buffalo or cow milk, prepared in different forms of *bocconcini* (morsels) or *treccie,* (braids); various types of pecorino; a fresh goat cheese called *caprino,* often flavored with pimpernel and other herbs; to the whole family of *provolone,* a spicy and sharp cheese made from fresh ewe's milk and curdled with lambs' rennet.

Coastal Campania enjoys an important and quantitative fishing industry. Over fifty percent of the catch consists of deep sea fish or blue water fish, particularly anchovy, sardine, and mackerel. Less important, but always available in every restaurant, are gilt-heads and red mullets that enrich restaurant grills filled with colorful squids, cuttlefish, and crustaceans of all sorts.

More than any other regional cuisine in Italy, Neapolitan cooking has produced dishes that have been adopted throughout the world—namely spaghetti and pizza. The use of the freshest ingredients of unequalled taste turns a plate of spaghetti with tomato sauce and basil, or a simple pizza *Margherita,* into an unforgettable gustatory experience.

In addition to the local varieties of *crostini,* a genuine antipasto is *Peperoni farciti,* peppers stuffed with a number of different ingredients: olives, capers, parsley, anchovies, or eggplant (or aubergines) and tomatoes. Sometimes the peppers are also stuffed with short pieces of boiled pasta, seasoned with a simple sauce. An interesting first course is the *Pasta*

ammiscata, or mixed pasta, made from all kinds of different leftovers from the bottom of pasta packages. This unusual mixture is sometimes presented in a picturesque manner by aesthetically conscious cooks and cooked and served in a creamy *cannellini* or white bean soup. Other first courses include pizzas, from the uncomplicated yet delicious *Margherita,* made with mozzarella, tomatoes, and basil, to the *Pizza Napoli* with anchovies added, to any of the many elaborate concoctions imagined by the quick-witted *pizzaioli,* or pizzamakers. As a second course, try the *Frutti di Mare,* or fruits of the sea, consisting of all imaginable fish, squid, and crustaceans served either cold or hot; or any of the delicious fish dishes such as *Cencenielli* (which literally means tiny chick peas), miniscule fish fried with a flour and butter batter, and sometimes placed on a pizza. For another variation of the second course, try the chewy yet light *Mozzarella in carrozza,* slices of mozzarella cheese between two slices of bread, dusted with flour, dipped in beaten eggs and then fried. For dessert finish with a slice of the traditional *pastiera* which symbolizes Naples the same way *panettone* symbolizes Milan or the *panforte* Siena. It is a sinfully luscious cake made of fresh ricotta cheese, chopped candied fruit, eggs, sugar, and sometimes chocolate morsels.

The white wines of this region are strong and robust, excellent with fish or soups. The most famous red or white wines of this region are the dry *Lacrima Christi* (or tears of Christ), made from the grapes grown on the southern slopes of Mount Vesuvius. Another heady and highly praised white wine is the *Ischia Bianco,* considered *da tutto pasto* but especially good with any fish.

Sicily

Sicilian cuisine is rich in a variety of fresh seafood. This pasta dish is served with a spicy tomato sauce in which giant prawns have been simmering.

Sicilian cuisine is one of the richest and most imaginative in Italy. This is due in part to the immense variety of products grown locally, but largely to the thousands of years of influence and occupation by many different and diverse civilizations. Over two million metric tons of citrus fruits are grown on Sicily every year, including unique blood oranges, lemons, mandarins, and grapefruits; one million tons of hard corn; six hundred thousand tons of other fruits and vegetables; and four hundred thousand tons of tomatoes. The quantity of olive oil and livestock production is constantly increasing, while the more traditional crops of pistachio and carob are decreasing in accordance to demand. In addition to the produce provided from the surrounding sea, these ingredients constitute the essential elements of Sicilian cooking. Sicilian pork products also have their own noteworthy characteristics, as the pigs on this island feed on a diet of acorns and prickly pears. The tradition of savory cooked sausages, rather than raw salami, lives on in this sunny and hot island. Among the many meat dishes the most singular is young, tender goat cooked in the *sciusciareddu* manner—stewed with tomatoes, artichokes, and asparagus, and available in almost all the characteristic restaurants. In addition to a number of delicious meat conserves are those made of tuna, eggs, or sardines. *Bottarga,* or salted tuna eggs which are dried in the sun in their original sack, are grated onto steaming spaghetti, making a culinary treat for the palate of any adventurous epicure.

The Sicilian meal begins with a parade of antipasti usually consisting of numerous vegetables displayed on a large table at the entrance of many restaurants. A wonderful antipasto is *pomodori ripieni,* raw tomatoes cut in half and stuffed with a scrumptious mixture of chopped *bottarga,* olives, and scampi. As a first course one must taste the celebrated *pasta con le sarde,* spaghetti boiled in salted water and flavored with fennel. Once the pasta is drained, chopped, and cleaned, sardines are added. Then the whole mixture is passed into a pan already containing oil, capers, more wild fennel, anchovy paste, pepper, pinoli nuts, raisins, chopped onions, and minced almonds. Sicily offers infinite variations on the theme of spaghetti and macaroni (short tubes of pasta), so much so that many restaurants often list only pasta with an incredible variety of sauces. As a second course the vegetable-based dishes are outstanding: numerous entreés based on eggplant or aubergine, often stuffed with sauces of onions and tomato, *caciocavallo* and other cheeses, or with mixed stuffings of vegetables, fish or minced meat; roasted or stuffed tomatoes, or fried or stewed artichokes.

Sicilian confectionary reflects a heritage of strong Eastern influences. *Cassata* must be tasted at least once. It is a light, layered sponge cake filled with sugared ricotta, which has been flavored either with cinnamon, vanilla, chocolate, or pistachio, and covered with a glaze of sugar onto which each cook creates elaborate fantasies of candied fruits, marron glacé, and other confections.

These colorful, hand-painted Sicilian liquor bottles adorn the windows of Taormina's local salumerias. The tall red bottle compares its contents to the volcanic "fire of Mt. Etna."

Chapter 4

Fashion

Sporting a white leather jacket, this woman walks along the Via Nationale, one of Rome's best streets for shopping.

The unconstructed look of this sweater and these trousers is a perfect example of Byblos' look of casual elegance. Note the clever contrast of texture and patterns.

Bruce Caines

The entire ensemble, from the tie to the briefcase, comes from Gucci, one of the leading fashion houses of Italy. Best known for their beautifully designed and crafted leather goods, Gucci is also prized for their classic, elegant, and expensive clothing.

Margaret Courtney-Clarke

FRETTE

ALL-ITALY

It's all in a name. Krizia, Valentino, Giorgio Armani, Laura Biagiotti, Fendi, Gianfranco Ferre', Gianni Versace. Whether it's haute couture or prêt à porter, the names mean everything. And in today's world of high fashion, the names to be reckoned with are Italian.

Claudia Cardinale isn't seen at the Venice film festival simply wearing a "dress," she's seen in a "Capucci." And anyone who's anyone knows it at a glance. The magazines even write that way. They'll show a photo of Cardinale

and Milan's famous fabrics, wool and leather were united in a successful post-war modernist movement which eventually grew to produce a generation of designers like Maiuccia Mandelli, the "godmother" of the new Milanese fashion, and creator of the house of Krizia.

Named after a famous character in Plato's dialogues, who was forever lavishing his wealth upon marvelous women, Krizia found almost instant success on the European and American markets.

The designers

looking stunning in sleeveless black, and the caption never fails to mention her favorite designer.

Fashion and celebrity go hand in hand. Styles may change with countless seasons, yet one thing is certain — Italian designers are the ones to watch.

It wasn't until after World War I that Italy began to seriously export an "Italian look." Up until then, Paris set the trends for most of the fashion conscious. Yet out of Milan came a prêt à porter, or ready-to-wear look, that was smart, distinctive, and thoroughly modern. It combined all the best elements of a classical style, and rapidly set trends for decades to come.

Modern, industrial Milan became the center for prêt à porter creations. Italian craftsmanship,

Mandelli's first ready-to-wear creations started coming out of Milan in the mid-fifties. With dresses and knitwear of remarkably simple line and shape, yet embellished with madcap details such as her famous animal motifs, Mandelli's clothes are known for their eccentricity and wit. Some of the more recent collections from Krizia look almost like futurist sculptures. Magnificent, yet accessible, her clothes are consistently popular.

Milan's most famous success story in men's and women's fashion is, of course, Giorgio Armani. Armani began as a buyer for men's wear in Milan in the fifties. His first collection for men appeared as recently as 1974, yet in little more than ten years, Armani's style is known almost everywhere.

His impact on design springs from an incredibly simple and sound concept. From the start, it was the premise of Armani's design to abolish the more standard conventions of the masculine look by steadily softening the stiff, virile lines of men's clothing. He took out the padding and the lining, and let the body define the line. Armani's clothes are loose and lightweight, and give an effortless look that is both elegant and comfortable.

His lines are structured with an easy softness, flawless tailoring, lightweight fabrics, and bright, warm hues. The Armani look is "style" without "structure," a faintly bohemian atmosphere of dress that turns a mildly disheveled look into something smart and fashionable.

Giorgio Armani's designs were an instant smash in the seventies when they began to appear in films like *Annie Hall* and *American Gigolo.* Armani's romance with Hollywood was cool, calculated, and unquestionably successful. Largely unknown at the time, he managed to design costumes for a number of American films, and it didn't hurt when actors like Jack Nicholson, Dustin Hoffman, Richard Gere, Woody Allen, and Diane Keaton all adopted the Armani look in their private lives.

Armani's collections for women are as successful as his things for men. Pants, big blouses, large flat-topped hats, and loosely draped jackets in linen, cotton, and silk, are all put together in diverse combinations for a simple mix and match approach to a comfortable yet exciting look.

More recently, Armani has translated his designs to knitwear and leather, and then further into the world of accessories, where, of course, there is absolutely no end.

While Milan is the capital for Italy's prêt à porter design, Flor-

Bruce Caines

The restrained elegance and ease of movement found in these Armani designs are the basis for his fashion philosophy.

Besides his couture and prêt-à-porter lines, Armani also produces a less expensive, more casual line of clothes, such as t-shirts, jeans, and sweat-clothes.

Margaret Courtney-Clarke

ence and Rome are the home of haute couture. Valentino is probably Rome's most famous designer. His bold, striking, utterly feminine creations affected an entire generation of designers.

Known for his incredibly elegant, sexy designs, Valentino pioneered his fashion concepts into a virtual empire worth over three hundred million dollars annually. Today, more than six thousand workers sew the Valentino label onto hundreds of his creations.

In the winter of 1983, Valentino was given a prestigious one-man retrospective at New York's Metropolitan Museum. Yet although his work had made it to the museums, Valentino's impact as a designer is far from over. He continues to turn out a spectacular array of haute couture creations, as well as lending his talents and resources to the Valentino Foundation, an organization founded to train and support a new generation of fashion designers.

A new generation of Italian designers are presently creating an impact on the fashion world. Gianfranco Ferre', whose first collection appeared in 1979, is certainly one of the leading new designers. Trained as an architect, Ferre's creations have a crisp, concise cut, creating a clearly defined silhouette. There is a geometry to his work which leads many people to describe his pieces as "hard-edged," while at the same time surprisingly "classical."

While the Italian designers are well-known for their women's clothes, the elegance, quality, and attractiveness of Italian menswear is unsurpassed in today's fashion.

As the ultimate women's couture designer, Valentino is known for fashion that is sophisticated, subtle yet unabashedly sexy.

Ferre' designs his clothing with an eye toward "style" rather than ever-changing "fashion." His concern for simplicity is revealed in the modern and streamlined cut of his clothes, and in the colors—sober dark grays, blacks, and greens, which are all juxtaposed with brilliant primary colors—fire engine red and tractor yellow. They're striking creations.

Another luminary in Italian fashion, Gianni Versace, creates fashions as sophisticated as those of Gianfranco Ferre', except that Versace's mood is completely different. He is a romantic. His clothes have a kind of rococo exuberance. Deceptively calm, with autumnal colors, smooth and undemonstrative, the Versace look is low-keyed, almost melancholic. His designs reflect the temperament of the dreamer. He's also something of a visionary among the current generation of designers. His neo-Grecian tunic dress has a feeling of supple elegance, superbly limp, with a look that's nearly timeless.

Of other Roman designers, Laura Biagiotti has found a place distinctly her own. Trained as an archeologist, Biagiotti got her start making prêt á porter for Capucci, Litirico, Bacocco, and Rive. Then, in 1972, Biagiotti came out with her first collection. She's known for making clothing both elegant and feminine—quilted jackets with floral patterns, luxurious cashmeres. It is said that when Biagiotti goes to work on a new collection she buries herself with a fierce resolve, doing her homework by digging deep into the rich past for her startling new look.

She works and lives outside of Rome, in a sixty-nine-room castle built in the eleventh century. Biagiotti bought her castle after her first early success, and it perfectly suits her personality as well as the

Svelte lines and soft, fluid fabric transform this man-tailored blazer into a dashing but definitely feminine look.

Bruce Caines

The classical motif of this Roman shop window exemplifies the fusion of the modern and the antique that is so omnipresent in Italian culture.

character of her designs.

Also from Rome is the famous Fendi family. A family business since 1918, Fendi is run by the five Fendi sisters, three of their husbands, and a number of their children.

Fendi found international attention when they introduced their first line of high fashion furs in 1955. Known for their unique colors, dramatic cuts and slashes, pleating, ruffles, and unconventional

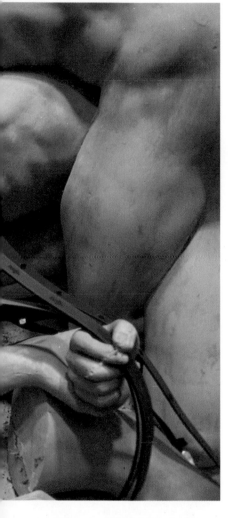

Even though Laura Biagiotti is known for her clothing, her line of sunglasses is also one of the most popular. Oversized, bold yet sleek, this pair makes a dramatic accessory.

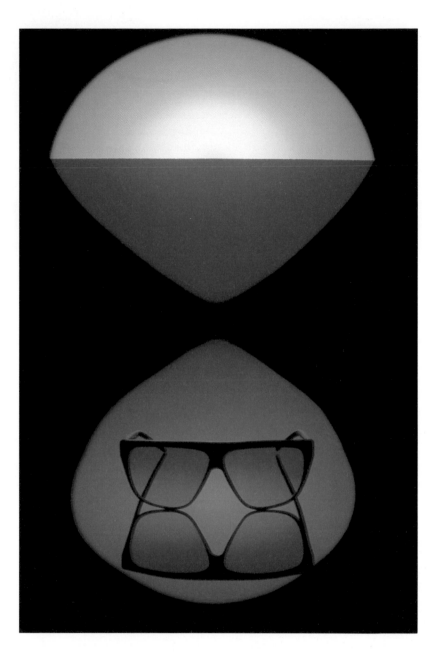

Fendi creations are designed by Karl Lagerfeld.

In speaking of the great Italian designers, one must mention Capucci and his "studio di forma." For more than forty years, Capucci has dedicated himself to fearless experiment with line, form, and color. His designs are never less than spectacular. More often, they border on the outrageous and fantastic. Capucci's shows are regarded almost as art exhibitions. He's been called the "Michelangelo of fashion," and is considered by some to be the last great original in fashion. As a designer, Capucci represents a style of elegance almost uniquely Italian. He's a master of taste, but more importantly, Capucci continues to create his timeless collections far outside the boundaries of passing trends. It's quite possible to say that this might be true of all the great modern Italian designers. It's what makes the Italian style so popular and, at the same time, distinctive—a seductive combination of flare, creativity, and character.

detailing, Fendi made their name by creating spectacular furs out of what was then known as "cast-off" material—undesirable fur because of color, size, or quality. Yet with bold, dramatic styling, the Fendi boutique on Rome's Via Borgogna grew ever more popular in the sixties and seventies. Fendi's famous "double F" logo found another expression when Fendi introduced their line of leather handbags and accessories. Many

FASHION

Shoes, Shoes, Shoes

In order to become a shoemaker in Venice, one first had to enter into a two-year apprenticeship under a "capo-mastro," a master craftsman. After apprenticing, if the worker sought to continue his trade, he was required to make three pairs of shoes, both men's and women's, to be judged before a group of the guild's most re-

Long curling toes were the vogue, as craftsmen began experimenting with the different hides of goat, sheep, calves, and buffalo. The wooden-heeled *chopine* was introduced, as well as the clog. Fashionable women in fifteenth century Venice were known to have worn heels on their shoes as high as sixty centimeters as a de-

Man's first vehicle was a simple pair of shoes. Thongs of leather that he strapped to his feet and left virtually unaltered as centuries rolled past.

The heel came and went. Even the "toe" was attached to various sandals and boots. Not until the twelfth century, in Venice, did the art of Italian shoemaking reach a pinnacle of prominence for which it's still famous.

In the early twelfth century, Venice was the supreme maritime power in the world. Her trade routes traveled far throughout distant China, Egypt, India, and Byzantium. Marco Polo had been to Kublai Khan's great capital of Khanbalik on the Yellow Sea, to Malacca, Calicut, Tabriz, and back. The Doge Dandola had left Venice on the Fourth Crusade in 1202, returning from Constantinople with treasures of gold-threaded fabrics, rare silks, damasks, and the four colossal horses of famous St. Mark's.

While the state of Venice revelled in her modern glory, elaborate artisan guilds were organized for the trades, each with a strict body of regulations meant to uphold the quality of Venetian goods.

spected shoemakers. If the shoes met their standard, the worker was given the State seal and the title of Venetian Shoemaker.

As Venice flourished, so did the art of shoemaking in Italy. The early shoes of this period were influenced by the style of footwear used by the Lombards during the seventh and eighth centuries, and the Romans, who of course borrowed nearly everything from the Greeks. The Lombards were famous for a traditional ceremony of symbolic recognition between father and son, whereby the son was asked to perform a solemn rite of passage by placing his foot into one of his father's shoes.

Ancient Etruscan, Egyptian, German, and Chinese footwear are all seen as early influences of this emerging Italian style. Tapestries, paintings, and mosaics from this period vividly document the varied and rapidly changing styles of footwear design.

mure means to avoid the muddy streets. Towering over their male counterparts by as much as a foot, they usually required the help of a servant merely to maneuver about.

It was the Spanish influence of the seventeenth century that brought Italian shoemaking into an age of elegance. High, graceful heels with satin and embroidery, velvet slippers with felt, silk, and jewels sewn into their surface made for sumptuous and elaborate designs that were high in demand in the capitals of Europe.

In 1773, the Republic of Venice had three hundred and forty shoemaker shops with over a thousand workers. With the fall of the Republic, the year 1797 saw a virtual end

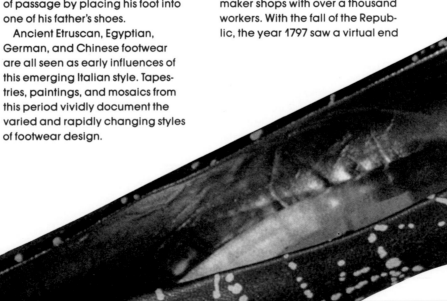

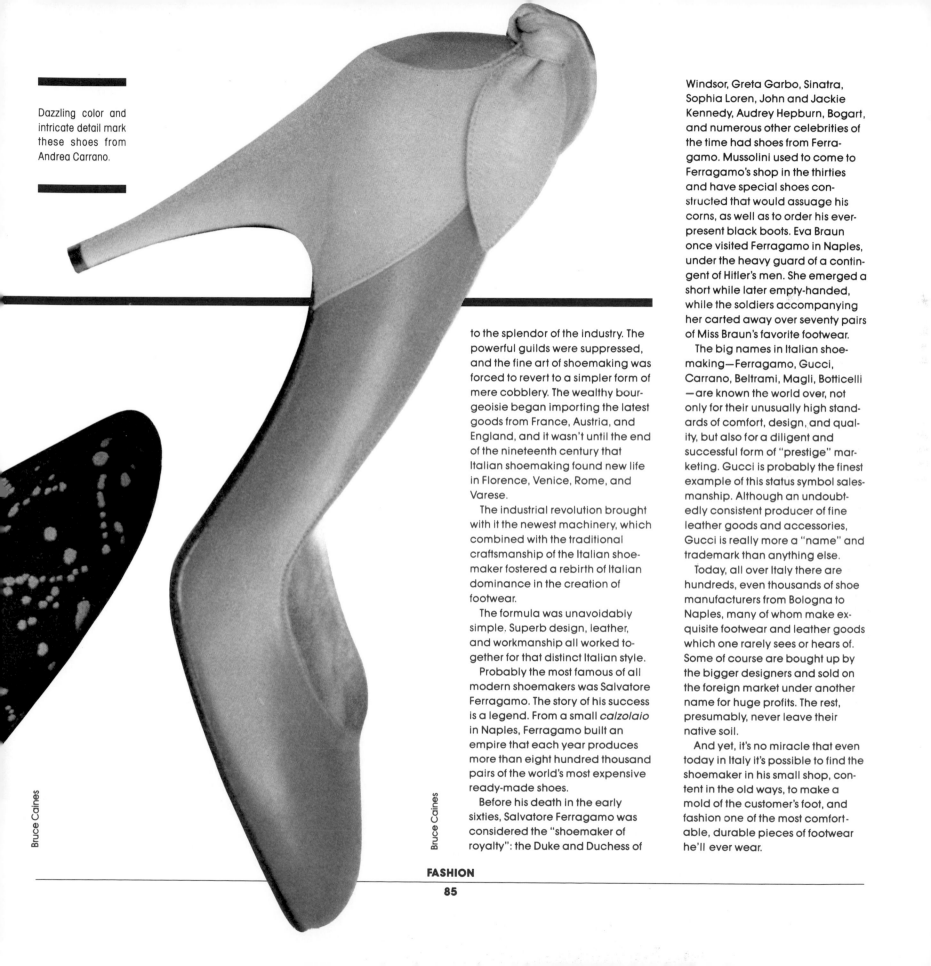

Dazzling color and intricate detail mark these shoes from Andrea Carrano.

Bruce Caines

Bruce Caines

Windsor, Greta Garbo, Sinatra, Sophia Loren, John and Jackie Kennedy, Audrey Hepburn, Bogart, and numerous other celebrities of the time had shoes from Ferragamo. Mussolini used to come to Ferragamo's shop in the thirties and have special shoes constructed that would assuage his corns, as well as to order his ever-present black boots. Eva Braun once visited Ferragamo in Naples, under the heavy guard of a contingent of Hitler's men. She emerged a short while later empty-handed, while the soldiers accompanying her carted away over seventy pairs of Miss Braun's favorite footwear.

The big names in Italian shoe-making—Ferragamo, Gucci, Carrano, Beltrami, Magli, Botticelli—are known the world over, not only for their unusually high standards of comfort, design, and quality, but also for a diligent and successful form of "prestige" marketing. Gucci is probably the finest example of this status symbol sales-manship. Although an undoubtedly consistent producer of fine leather goods and accessories, Gucci is really more a "name" and trademark than anything else.

Today, all over Italy there are hundreds, even thousands of shoe manufacturers from Bologna to Naples, many of whom make exquisite footwear and leather goods which one rarely sees or hears of. Some of course are bought up by the bigger designers and sold on the foreign market under another name for huge profits. The rest, presumably, never leave their native soil.

And yet, it's no miracle that even today in Italy it's possible to find the shoemaker in his small shop, content in the old ways, to make a mold of the customer's foot, and fashion one of the most comfortable, durable pieces of footwear he'll ever wear.

to the splendor of the industry. The powerful guilds were suppressed, and the fine art of shoemaking was forced to revert to a simpler form of mere cobblery. The wealthy bourgeoisie began importing the latest goods from France, Austria, and England, and it wasn't until the end of the nineteenth century that Italian shoemaking found new life in Florence, Venice, Rome, and Varese.

The industrial revolution brought with it the newest machinery, which combined with the traditional craftsmanship of the Italian shoemaker fostered a rebirth of Italian dominance in the creation of footwear.

The formula was unavoidably simple. Superb design, leather, and workmanship all worked together for that distinct Italian style.

Probably the most famous of all modern shoemakers was Salvatore Ferragamo. The story of his success is a legend. From a small *calzolaio* in Naples, Ferragamo built an empire that each year produces more than eight hundred thousand pairs of the world's most expensive ready-made shoes.

Before his death in the early sixties, Salvatore Ferragamo was considered the "shoemaker of royalty": the Duke and Duchess of

Margaret Courtney-Clarke

This precious ivory silk panel was woven in the late seventeenth century. The fastidious attention to detail and remarkable craftsmanship found in this piece are still apparent in today's silk industry.

Silk

As legend goes, it was in 2700 B.C. when the Empress Si-Ling-Chi, wife of Hoang Tee (inventor of the calendar), first began gathering thread from the cocoon of silkworms, and reeling the thread into continuous fiber.

The silkworm at the time was merely a common, hairless, yellowish caterpillar in northern Asia, whose life was spent feeding upon the mulberry tree. With the Empress's discovery, he began a coveted and pampered life, treasured throughout the world.

Since ancient times, both Italy and China have always had trees in the mulberry family. The black mulberry grew wild in Italy, and was later cultivated as an ornament in the gardens of palazzos and villas. But the silkworm didn't come to Italy until the tenth century, when the Byzantines brought the precious worm to Sicily. At the same time they introduced a different version of his favorite food — the white mulberry. The leaves of the Chinese white mulberry are known to have the most tender leaves, more delectable to the caterpillar. Fortunately, this tree was perfectly suited to a climate and soil where grapes are grown.

The Byzantines knew that the silkworm could easily thrive in a place like Italy, and once he was introduced to his new country, the manufacturing of silk in Italy took hold.

From Palermo to Messina, then north to Naples, Florence, Bologna, Modena, and finally Lombardy, Venice and Piemonte, the manufacture of silk gradually moved north over the centuries. (It's important to note that the artisans of this rare trade were mostly Jews. They were skilled craftsmen who adopted silk making and took it with them as they moved, handing down the secrets of the trade from generation to generation.)

While Italy today is the world's third largest producer of silk, she is ranked first in quality over both Japan and China. Most Italian silk comes from Como, in the Lombardy region. The *Comaschi*, as they are called, have elevated silk making to an art. The masterpieces of the Renaissance—opulent silk tapestries, silk fabric with gold and silver threads woven in—were all manufactured in and around this region.

The introduction in 1872 of the mechanical loom rapidly altered the Italian silk-making industry. In Como today, over 32,000 artisans work in a series of small factories in and around the lake.

Valentino, Krizia, Ungaro, Ferre', and virtually all the top Italian designers come to Como for their silk. The papal and cardinal robes of the Vatican are crafted in Como, as well as the flags of many nations.

The tradition of this fine Italian art is supported by the unceasing demand for the highest quality products. And while much of Italy's silk fabric is still handmade and printed exactly as it was a century ago, the silk makers of Como have also utilized the latest innovations in manufacturing.

Margaret Courtney-Clarke

Lush and luxurious, these richly decorated silk scarves by Gucci are a timeless accessory.

Fabrics

Bruce Caines

Italian fabrics are as famous for their beauty as they are for their quality. A label that says "Made in Italy" is a mark of prestige. Generation after generation, the highest standards of care and craftsmanship have been handed down with pride. While new methods and technologies are forever being utilized, the attitudes and traditions of Italian fabric manufacture and design have hardly changed at all.

In the region of Tuscany, the small city of Prato is responsible for most of Italy's modern textile production. For centuries, Prato has been known as the city of *stracci,* or rags. Today, truckloads of old clothing and fabrics are brought in daily to be recycled through a chemical process that burns the vegetable fibers in order to reclaim the original thread. The fabric manufacturers of Prato waste nothing in their work, which is why, for years, the Red Cross and other international charity organizations have continued to send thousands of tons of collected materials to be reprocessed by carbonization techniques. Prato's major product is a three-blend process of wool, acrylic, and polyester which is highly popular throughout the world. It's probably the most efficient and inexpensive form of fabric manufacture.

Further north in the region of Lombardy, is Como, Italy's silk center. The area around Lake Como is dotted with hundreds of small silk factories, none of which employ more than twenty or thirty workers, giving Como a reputation as the "China of Italy."

It is in Como that some of the world's most beautiful silks and velvets are created. Most of this silk work is still hand-printed and painted in the "plisse" style made popular by the Italian designer Fortuny. Yet more recently, the Comaschi began using a process of printed silk production that has created a fabric that can be washed in the same high temperatures as ordinary cotton. This has contributed considerably to the output of Como's silk manufacture, and in the last ten years many millions worth of velvet and silk has come from this region.

Yet in spite of this increase in production, the quality control of the Como factories is most rigorous. It can require up to three days of labor to produce only thirty meters, or a *pezza* of silk, which is part of the reason this region maintains the reputation it's had since the days of Marco Polo.

Italian wool comes from the Piedmont area, from the city of Biella. Generation after generation of the *Biellesi* are still handing down their old style tradition of woolmaking. This area is also famous for new innovations in other fields of textile technology. In Biella they produce a cashmere that rivals any from England, and their wools are considered to be equal or even superior to those made in Scotland.

Leather Goods and Accessories

Bruce Caines

This artfully designed pocketbook is made with supple leather and superb skill as are most Italian leather goods.

Italy exports billions of dollars worth of leather goods and accessories every year. Sixty percent of the handbags manufactured in Italy are made for the foreign market. Shoes, wallets, satchels, briefcases, gloves, boots, suitcases, and belts, not to mention Italy's famously stylish leather jackets, skirts, and pants, are considered without question the finest leather goods in the world.

It's an age-old tradition of quality that has continued largely unaltered for centuries. Except for the occasional introduction of modern machinery in some of the sewing and tanning processes, a great deal of the work is still done by hand.

The centers of the leather industry reside in Florence, Naples, Vincencza, Modena, Venice, Varese, and Milan, exactly where they flourished in all their Renaissance glory. The product of each of these areas is characterized by three primary styles of leatherwork, formerly distinguished by the ancient political and geographical divisions of the nation: the "Florentine style"— sober and classical, almost formal in demeanor; "Neapolitan style"—more colorful and decorative with Spanish and Islamic roots; and the old "Venetian

Textured white
leather distin-
guishes this Gucci
handbag.

style"—a wonderful synthesis of the Arabic and the Byzantine, fused with engravings and impressions with traces of gold in its elaborate toolwork.

These schools of leatherwork characterize much of what is produced in Italy today, yet leather goods have also set new trends distinctive in style; fashion with an almost personal approach. Today the most innovative designers of leather goods, whether shoes, handbags, coats, or belts, come out of Italy.

The big names in leather and accessories are of course Gucci, Fendi, Ferragamo, Botticelli, Beltrami, and others. Although they control a sizable portion of the foreign market with their exports, these firms make up only a small percentage of Italy's entire leather industry.

Just as in the Renaissance days of the ancient guilds, Italy is still made up of thousands of small craftsmen and designers. One hardly hears of these people, but they continuously create marvelous goods. This rich legacy, largely handed down from generation to generation, allows many craftsmen to do the leather tanning processes, the cutting, skinning, and lasting, with the same skill and formula as their ancestors used during the fifteenth century.

Even the large leather goods firms are essentially "families." Ferragamo is family-owned in Florence. Gucci is still run by the "godfather" of the prominent family. And Fendi is controlled by the five Fendi sisters. It's exactly this sort of tightknit tradition and skill constantly assures an unusually high quality of goods.

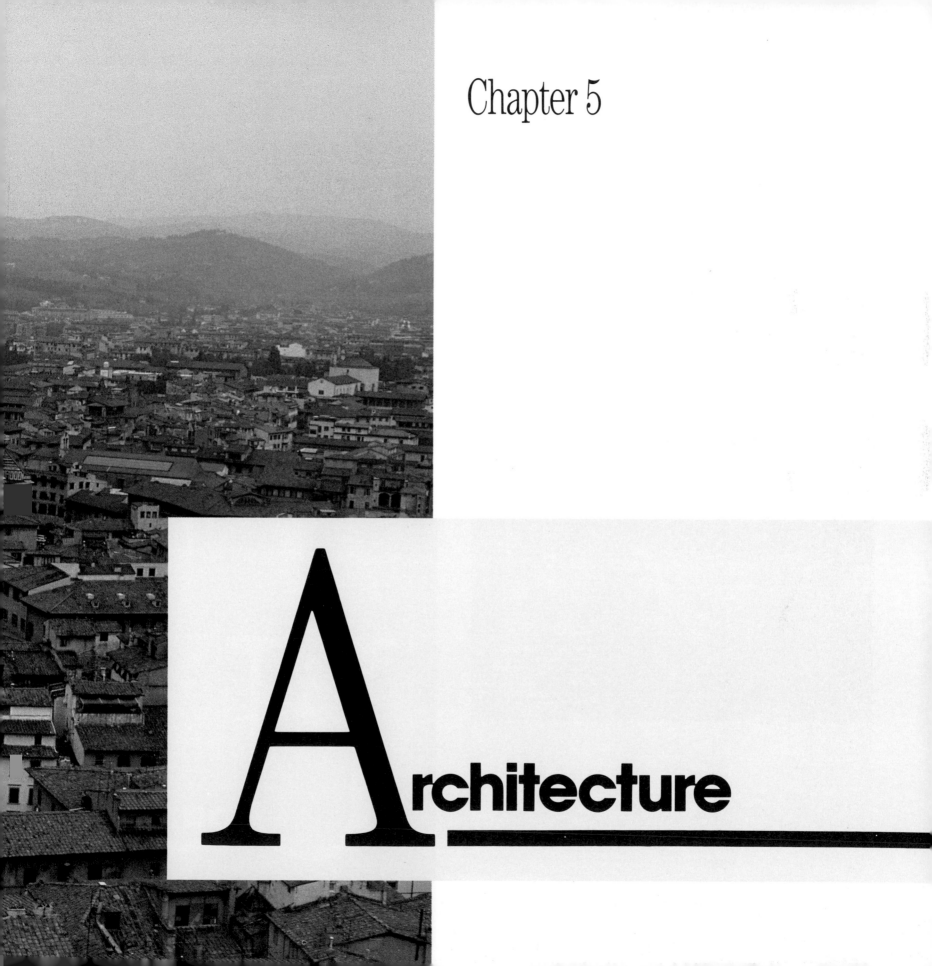

Chapter 5

Architecture

Many of Italy's streets look like this one in Perugia, virtually unchanged since medieval times.

Margaret Courtney-Clarke

The only bridge in Florence that escaped the bombings of WWII, the Ponte Vecchio is also the oldest. Today visitors can admire the artistry of the many gold- and silversmiths who work on the bridge and its ethereal beauty.

Margaret Courtney-Clarke

A stroll through an Italian city constitutes a sort of urban archaeology, a walk through time in which monuments of every epoch are juxtaposed and form unforgettable harmonies and contrasts. Artifacts of the ancient Roman past are to be found everywhere in Italy. But the roots of the modern Italian city undoubtedly lie in the medieval, Renaissance, and baroque peri-

Urban Spaces

ods. Each of these epochs imposed its unique ideal of urban form, adding its own spatial orientation to that pre-existing.

In the course of the Middle Ages, the populace turned from a feudal, agricultural lifestyle and began to assemble in cities, centers of commerce and learning. In form, the medieval Italian city is winding and maze-like. Logical order of streets and squares is not to be found. The shape of the city is random, growing organically from the needs of the populace. In Venice, Florence, Perugia, and Siena, all commercial powers and centers of culture in the medieval period, streets, squares, and structures began to emerge in a pattern which reflected the lifestyles and needs of the time. In Venice, for example, the alleys and narrow streets of Santa Maria Formosa (begun in 1175) form "outdoor interiors," that sprang up in response to the commercial activities which took place there. Medieval Venice is a city of great visual variety, with the changing reflections of water emphasizing the diversity of buildings tall and small, streets crooked and straight.

The daunting perspective of Piazza San Marco, Venice's glorious square.

The medieval sections of Florence are also meandering. The Piazza Della Signoria, the central square in Florence, is conveniently connected to a crooked passageway that leads to the Arno, again a response to the needs of trade. The winding streets of Perugia twist and turn around the natural relief of the rural hilltop upon which it was built. Fourteenth century Siena represents the culmination of medieval city planning with its system of triple city squares. The central square was the site of civic authority and government, a place of justice. The second square was the marketplace, exalting the strength of the new economic society. Finally, the sacred square of the cathedral represented the power of the Church, the pivotal role played by religion in the daily life of the people.

The planning of Siena foreshadowed the logic and geometry which dominated the Renaissance ideal of the city. The cities of the Renaissance were revolutionized by the new influence of mathematics. Cities were organized around the concept of perspective; specific focal points were used to impose compact, clear, and balanced shapes on the winding medieval streets. Thus, the massive

Montefeltro Palace of Urbino, known as a "city in the shape of a palace," stands high above the other city structures, establishing a spatial focus with its vast quadrangle, designed by Luciano Laurana in 1465. Geometrical design with an eye to perspective is also present in Renaissance Venice, where the two adjacent trapezoids of St. Mark's Square serve to draw the viewer's attention to the activity of the Lagoon. Ferrara, too, had to accommodate a tortuous medieval urban nucleus. Known as the artist of angles, Biaggio Rosetti reorganized the city center around the Palazzo Diamanti, the faceted Renaissance palace which became a focal point of the city in 1492

Whereas the Renaissance favored an ordered and geometrically pleasing city, the baroque masters of the seventeenth century created grandiose and theatrical designs. In the late sixteenth century, Michelangelo pointed the way to baroque urban planning by opening and consolidating the space among the massive buildings of Rome's Capitoline Hill, using giant pilasters to join the structures for spectacular effect. The baroque Piazza di Spagna in Rome similarly serves as a magnetic convergence point of streets, all leading to the dramatic cascade of Bernini's Fountain of Barracia. The urban planning of which Bernini, Borromini, and Guarini were the baroque masters is astounding in its dynamic openness, its mood of largesse and movement, its union of curvilinear buildings and vast space. The baroque city planners emphasized the effects of vista. The Piazza del Quirinale in Rome, for example, is defined by the oblique facades of palaces and allows for an opening on one side to the majestic Strada Pia, while on the other there is a grandiose view of St. Peter's Basilica.

Margaret Courtney-Clarke

The interior courtyard of Milan's Brera Art Academy evokes a contemplative and serene mood.

The monuments of Italy are of two predominant types, the palaces and villas in which the wealthy and powerful lived, and the churches built for the glorification of God. Testaments of man's spirituality, his will to separate himself from the mundane and center himself In enduring and transcendental beauty, Italian churches take a variety of forms. They range from the severe and humble to the rich and flamboyant.

An ancient prototype for Catholic church building was the Roman Pantheon (27 B.C.-118 A.D.), temple of all the gods, a vast, domed affair which oould hold an enormous number of worshippers beneath its vault. With the rising popularity

The Churches of Italy

One of the tallest cathedrals in Italy, Milan's Duomo has been called overwrought by some critics.

The interior of St. Peter's in Rome was designed to inspire awe and elicit spiritual ecstacy. Note the drama of the light that illuminates Bernini's *baldacchino* (altar).

and toleration of Christianity in Rome during the reign of the Emperor Constantine (280-337 A.D.), churches were erected to serve the newly converted. The long, rectangular basilica with a broad, central nave leading to the altar was the most popular style for early church building. St. Peter's Basilica, the church of the papacy, was begun as early as 330 A.D. This center of Catholicism was reconstructed in the sixteenth century, with the greatest Renaissance artists collaborating on its design. Michelangelo designed St. Peter's grandiose cupola, recalling and outstripping the domed Pantheon of imperial Rome.

The charm of Italian cities lies in the coexistence of these diverse modes and styles of spatial organization. There is a magical sense of freedom involved in following the skein of meandering medieval streets and then chancing upon an imposing baroque square or the ingenious symmetry of a Renaissance facade. The centuries have consecrated all of these forms, which create a unique interplay of beauty in which modern buildings may be incorporated. The train station of Florence, constructed in 1936, a massive metal building noted for its staid horizontality, stands as an assertion of modernity near the historic Romanesque church, Santa Maria Novella. The new buildings of the University of Urbino, designed by Giancarlo di Carlo in the mid-sixties, constitute a sensitive, delicate insertion of a modern urban environment in the midst of a magnificent old city.

The great lesson of the Italian city, urban space in which life has prevailed for long centuries, is that continuity allows for diversity. The human spirit is as multifarious as its significant monuments.

At the time of Constantine, the Roman Empire had been split into two parts, the western empire centered in Rome and the eastern empire, Byzantium, with its capital city of Constantinople. The Byzantine style was both opulent and exotic, characterized by soaring and billowing domes, seemingly weightless vaults of stone hovering above silent space. Covered with glittering mosaics reflecting the light of countless candles, these Byzantine interiors were mystical and other-worldly. The Byzantine style was early imported into Italy and some of the finest examples are found in the northern city of Ravenna. The church of San Appolinare (505 A.D.) is prized for precious mosaics depicting a hieratic procession of saints and rulers, their movement caught in a mysterious stasis. The consummate example of Byzantine splendor in Italy is, of course, found in the design of St. Mark's in Venice, begun in 1063. Planned in the shape of a Greek cross and surmounted by five domes, St. Mark's is a radiant monument of man's quest for the metaphysical. The gilded and luxurious church, sated with light, is a luminous haven for the spirit but also attests to the commercial power of the ruler of the Adriatic.

In contrast to the opulent orientalism of the Byzantine style, a more severe and compact architecture was favored in Lombardy in the second half of the eleventh century. Also in Florence, the logical concerns of the Renaissance were pre-figured in the Romanesque church of San Mineato (1018-1063), a structure which is solid, horizontal, and close to the earth. Yet, with its delicate stonework and painted facade, San Mineato is also a graceful structure which seems a splendid portal, a welcoming and ornamental gateway to paradisal joy. Responding to humanistic ideals of balance and decorum, the Florentine Renaissance

Margaret Courtney-Clarke

brought forth many geometrically oriented churches, among them Filippo Brunelleschi's octagonal Santa Maria del Fiore (1418-36), Florence's "Duomo." The harmony of this Renaissance church tends to induce a mood of contemplative quiescence in the worshipper, a sense of equipoise between the physical and the spiritual.

Rather than calm contemplation, baroque architects strove to create a mood of spiritual exaltation in the worshipper by introducing dynamic movement into the church interior. Baroque artists brought the concept of infinity within the grasp of the devout by creating optical illusions of seemingly endless space in their churches. Using a system of ellipses, Borromini made the small dome of San Carlino in Rome (1633-35) appear a limitless point of ascension into heaven. Bernini's Roman baroque church of San'Andrea (1658) or Longherra's Santa Maria della Salute in Venice (1631-87) are theatrical spaces in which altars serve as stages for the drama of the Mass, and ceilings are transformed into heavens teeming with angels. The baroque church in Italy epitomizes the interrelationship of the material and the immaterial, the sumptuousness of the building provoking metaphysical experience. Italian churches are remote from the Puritan ethic. They are places of supreme and infinite beauty which demonstrate the divine spark of human creativity.

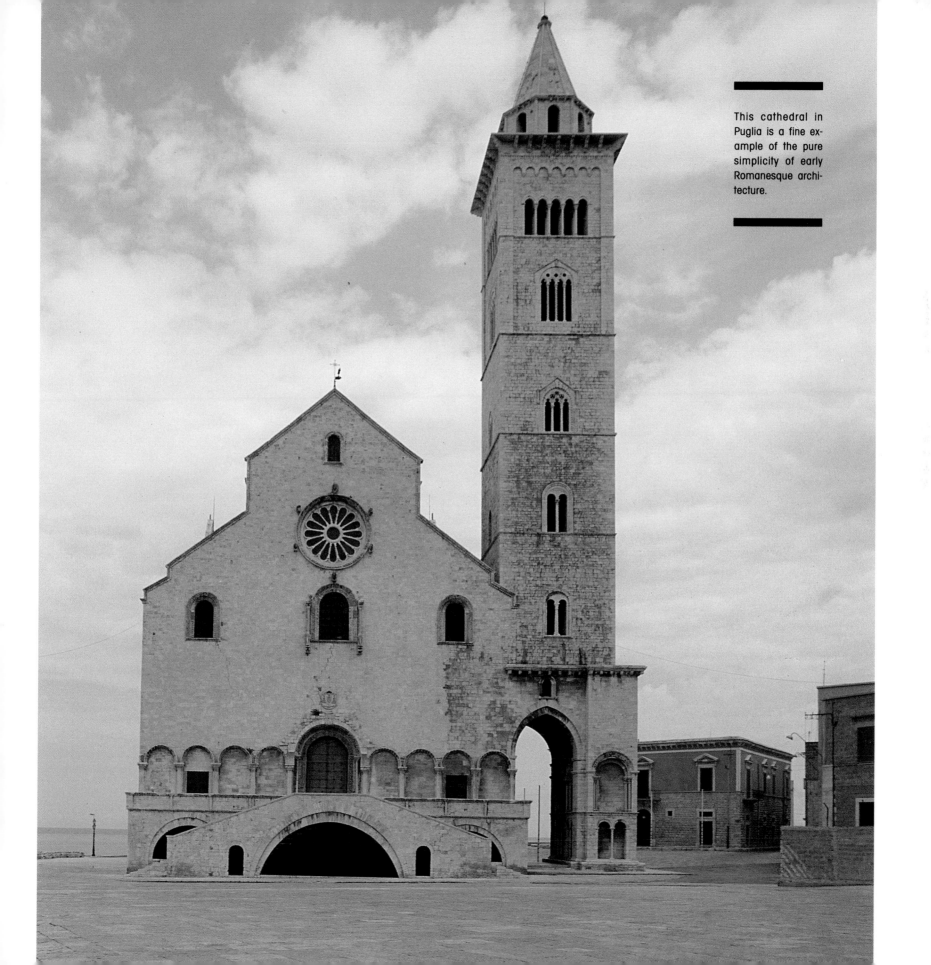

This cathedral in Puglia is a fine example of the pure simplicity of early Romanesque architecture.

Palaces and Villas

The grand approach to this private villa heightens the anticipation of the visitor.

Italian palaces and villas conjure thoughts of warm stone and sun-gilded colors. These are retreats of pleasure, where the nobility could indulge in a life of cultured ease amidst exquisite harmonies of architecture and landscape. One need only recall the imposing Farnese Palace in Rome. Built in the late fifteenth century for a wealthy papal family, the Farnese was famed for its library of Greek manuscripts, its collection of ancient sculpture, and its frescoed gallery of mythological erotica painted by Annibale Carracci.

Behind an impenetrable, fortress-like facade, the Ducal Palace of Urbino concealed an interior design of finesse and luxury, a world of sculpted putti and painted muses. Here, the Montefeltro family could rule and discuss the finer points of love and good manners while wandering the shade of a secret garden ornamented with cascading fountains and statuary recalling the classical past.

Like the ancient Romans retreating from the city to their private villas in resorts such as Pompeii and Armerina, the Italian nobility of the fifteenth century discovered the virtues of pastoral life. Inspired by the prevailing humanist philosophy which exalted the wonder of nature, noble families fled the bustle of the cities and demanded self-sufficient homes in isolated environments. Initially, the design of these country homes combined elements from great rural farmhouses, fortresses, and convents, but soon the classical prototypes of imperial Rome became dominant. The definitive example of the humanist dwelling is the Tuscan Medici Villa in Poggio a Caiano, built

Painted *grottesche* enliven this fifteenth-century palazzo in Pavia's Piazza Ducale.

by Giuliano da Sangallo in 1480. Its monumental facade, complete with front portico and ground-floor terraces overlooking gardens, encloses an interior of grand salons with frescoes by Jacopo Pontormo.

With the strengthening of papal power and patronage in the sixteenth century, architectural classicism further matured. The great minds of the day elaborated theories of perspective and interior space. Thus, Bramante, Peruzzi, and Raphael collaborated on Cardinal Giulio de Medici's Villa Madama outside of Rome. Now owned by the state, the vast structure has been recently renovated, revealing the full beauty of its curved and projecting portico, its luminous loggia commanding the landscape. Similarly, in Pesaro, Girolamo Genga designed l'Imperiale for Eleonora Gonzaga, one of the most powerful women of the sixteenth century. Her villa has the cool, intellectual elegance favored by the Mannerist school. Like the Villa Madama, it is harmoniously integrated with a surrounding forest, a jewel inserted in a worthy setting.

In the ever unique Venice, cluster of 117 islands isolated in a lagoon, space was at a premium and palaces existed side by side in the closest community. Often, the palaces of several families would share a common facade and waterways. Among the most beautiful of the Venetian palaces are the C'a d'Oro, the stonework of which resembles the most fragile lace, the Contarini, with its exterior spiralling staircase, and the Barbaro, which inspired memorable passages in Henry James's *The Wings of a Dove*. Like the Florentines and the Romans, the Venetians also desired their autonomous country seats surrounded by gardens, a great

Crowning a hilltop with its sublime perfection in Vicenza, Palladio's Villa Rotunda is one of the architect's greatest achievements.

luxury in the city of stone and water. The region of Stra and the Brenta Road between Venice and Padua were privileged sites for private estates, and Andrea Palladio was a favored architect. Palladio's *Four Books* spread throughout Europe, establishing respect for plane geometry, function, and an integral relationship between exterior and interior design. The interior of Palladio's Villa Barbaro in Maser (1557–1558) is adorned with frescoes by the Venetian, Paolo Veronese, which begin in the salon and proceed without interruption to the adjoining rooms. Palladio's masterpiece is the Villa Rotunda in Vicenza, a lyric interior

of sloping curves and majestic columns. Crowning a hilltop with its solitary perfection, the Rotunda has four separate loggias overlooking the horizon.

One of the most significant products of seventeenth century architecture, the Palazzo Barberini near Rome, was completed in 1627. The Baroque sculptor and architect, Giovanni Bernini, constructed a set of sequential facades which project outward to define the courtyard and an interior salon of astonishing proportion, eighteen meters high.

A century later, architects eschewed such grandiose effects, favoring instead interior comfort

and playful decoration. Ceilings were lowered and rooms lengthened in the eighteenth century, for example in the Villa Favorita by Ferdinando Fuga (1768), with its fan-shaped staircase, rococo stucco work, and luxurious furnishing.

In the three hundred years between the fifteenth and eighteenth centuries, constants in Italian villa construction were a sense of symmetry and peace. There was a poetic integration of home and natural surroundings conducive to the leisured and intellectual life favored by the humanist nobility. The aristocracy prized its isolation and cultivated their homes as refuges of art and distinction.

Behind an impenetrable fortress-like facade, the Ducal Palace of Urbino conceals an interior of exquisite luxury.

A white peacock adds further visual impact to the already baroque gardens of the Palazzo Borromeo on the Isola Bella in Lago Maggiore.

The Fantastic Gardens

Italian gardens constitute a major chapter in the history of architecture. Whether artistically intricate or artificially geometric, lyric or prosaic, they are fragments of a world created solely from man's imagination. Although a popular activity, gardening is generally associated with the gentility of the bourgeoisie villa, the grounds of the aristocrat's palace or chateau, or the mystical atmosphere of a monastery. The garden is an artistic celebration of the marriage between that which is crafted and that which is natural. The art form emerged in response not only to man's visual appetite, but also to the ancient need to tame the wild, to establish a secure and fluent dialogue with natural surroundings. Springing from agricultural regions, gardening was born in the orchards and vegetable plots, where the creative act of choosing the best produce as well as designing its order and placement in the soil, came into play. The history of gardening is varied and complex, the result of many

Symmetrical, harmonious, and rational, the gardens of Villa Bagnaia in Viterbo are a spectacular example of Renaissance design.

Margaret Courtney-Clarke

sometimes contradictory influences. Geographic variety and climatic differences caused the cultural, social, and territorial conceptions of the south to differ greatly from the central and northern regions of Italy. The gardens and orchards on the coast of Sicily were jealously guarded in order to protect valuable shade and became private sanctuaries for their owners. Dating from medieval times, gardens of the central and northern Italian regions were usually the work of a single author. These gardeners produced reflective works of art worthy of a study all their own.

Popular with the ancient Romans, gardens went from being the local creations of artisans to spectacular scenic landscapes reflecting the spatial grandiosity of the Hadrianic era. With his idea of creating a "villa in the shape of a city," Hadrian built a microcosm at Tivoli (118–138 A.D.) with an organic weaving of stone and green hedges modelled after Pompeii and Herculaneum. However, with the fall of the Roman Empire, all methods of Roman artistic design disappeared in Europe. Marshes, swamps, and overgrown pastures replaced the sculpted green gardens of Rome as towns gradually

Italian gardens were designed for more than contemplative retreats. Some have more than a hint of mischief and playfulness as seen here in this "monster garden" near Viterbo.

Margaret Courtney-Clarke

became isolationist and xenophobic. Groups of houses sprang up surrounding orchards and vegetable plots in a lean attempt at self-sufficiency. Only in the Middle Ages with the influence of the Middle East did monastic cloister gardens fill with aromatic and medicinal plants, fruits and vegetables, and thus begin a revival of the ancient art of gardening. As a result of the Islamic influence, the regions of Sicily and the Amalfi coast began to take advantage of the natural beauty and sunny climate of their regions. Unusual artistic efforts combined with the presence of citrus fruits and vegetables produced fabulous, exotic garden panoramas. Two examples of this fruition of gardening are the Villa Rufolo in Ravello on the Gulf of Salerno (eleventh to twelfth centuries), and the Small Cloister of Paradise (1103) adjacent to the Cathedral of Amalfi, stupendous in the lyric simplicity of its design. In the north, gardens of herbs, fruits, and flowers in the shape of labyrinths were built throughout the fourteenth century for the nobles of Lucca, Verona, Pavia, and Milan.

The gardens of the fifteenth century gradually evolved into more "anti-naturalistic" settings, with an emphasis on a more sculpted and disciplined look, beautiful in a man-made, artificial sense. Hydraulic and other techniques were employed by architects to create "gardens of delectation," shaped hedges in the form of palaces, pruned laurels in geometric shapes that traced passageways resembling city streets. A symbol of the dominant classes, agricultural territories were transformed into microcosms for the nobility. The Medici dominion in 1456 consisted of fifty villas, among them: Cafaggiolo, Trebbi, and Careggi, "signed" by Michelozzo; Poggio a Caiano, located between Flor-

ence and Prato, designed by Giuliano da Sangallo for Lorenzo the Magnificent.

Characterized by strong geometric determinism, obsessive attention to symmetry, and at times monotonously green, the gardens of the sixteenth century were often static and uniform. From the generous prototypes of Raphael's Villa Madama in Rome, the Farnesina Chigi by Peruzzi, and the Palazzo del Te in Mantova by Giulio Romano, from this irresistible fascination with crafting land into artistic expression, sprang the so-called "Italian Garden." Destined for great popularity, in reality it was a mortifying attempt to crystallize the environment, a devitalizing rather than invigorating view of nature. The Boboli Gardens in Florence by Tribolo, and the ostentatious Villa d'Este in Tivoli by Pirro Ligorio are both of the second half of the sixteenth century. They are scenic visions, voluminous and monochromatic with playful fountains of water which "enchant but do not persuade—ripped out as they are from their natural context." (B. Zevi) However, the seductive Villa Foscari in the town of Gamberare di Mira near Venice (1559–60) designed by Andrea Palladio, is of a very different temperament. Characterized by their spaciousness, these gardens allow the reflection of light and the presence of the river Brenta to render it less static and still elegant.

The dazzling gardens of the baroque and late baroque periods are characterized by multidirectional plots, distant foci, and a nervous adherence to natural dynamics. The outskirts of Rome are populated by numerous villas and gardens of monumental stature (Mondragone, Ludovisi, and Falconieri). One of these, the Aldobrandi park in Frascati (1598–1604) is choreographed and at times quite verbose, but, nevertheless is sensibly fused with the natural landscape. The villas of Lombardy of this era are sumptuously located on beautiful lakes. Villa Carlotta on Lake Como (eighteenth century), "dressed" with azaleas and rhododendrons, and the exquisite Isola Bella (1622–71), festively anchored in Lake Maggiore, are both good examples of the baroque garden.

The eighteenth century is strikingly contradictory. While the architecture of this century is characterized by strict neoclassic solemnity, the squares, parks, and gardens are gloriously varied. Especially notable are the regions of Piedmont, Campania, and Sicily. The Palazzina de Caccia near Turin (1729–36) by Iuvarra, for example, incorporates various French elements and establishes a rich and variegated dialectic with nature. The awkwardly shaped Reggia of Caserta (1752–74) by Vanvitelli is an example of late classicism. Along the Vesuvian coast, in the region of Campania, luxurious gardens abound: Barra, St. George in Cremano, and Torre del Greco are elegantly linked to the magnificent Favorita (circa 1768, di F. Fuga) in Resina near Portici. Sicilian villas and their gardens, immortalized by the classic novel, *Il Gattopardo (The Leopard)*, are predominantly shaped by the exuberant movement of the terrain.

The eclectic nineteenth century offered a virtuosity in both public and private design. In Rome, the art of gardening culminates in the creation of the gardens on the slopes of the Pincio. The transformation of the Piazza del Popolo of Valadier and the park Villa Torlonia, designed by Giuseppe Jappelli, employs a dissonant rhapsody of beautiful constructions which denote the advent of modernity.

The maze-like design of this topiary is reminiscent of the great gardens of Versailles. These gardens are adjacent to the Villa Gamberaia in Florence.

Ten Architects, Ten Great Events

Italian architecture is rich with a great quantity and quality of work which even in its oldest or most anonymous forms can be seen as revolutionary, capable of inspiring new artistic languages. It is possible, in fact, to trace an itinerary through the peninsula that highlights ten fundamental works by ten great architects which serve to usher in the modern era. Five of these are true titans of their craft, working at various times from the late Middle Ages, early Renaissance, and through to the paroxysm of the baroque era: the Palazzo Vecchio, by Arnolfo di Cambio, Santo Spirito, by Brunelleschi, the Laurentian Library, by Michelangelo, il Redentore, by Palladio, and S. Ivo, by Borromini. The remaining five are singular artists—unique, less imitated than the first five, but just as forward in their architectural thinking. From an artist with mannerist tendencies, to the subtle, graphic outlook of an "outsider" like Piranesi, to a twentieth century architect stigmatized by the noisy intervention of the past, they have all greatly influenced the course of architectural history: the Palazzo Massimo, by Peruzzi, Palazzo del Te, by Giulio Romano, Le Carceri d'Invenzioni, by Piranesi, La Casa del Fascio, by Terragni, and the restructuring of the Castelvecchio in Verona by Scarpa.

The clean, imposing lines of Arnolfo Cambio's Palazzo Vecchio translate into an almost modern sensibility. This building is the pivotal focus of Florence.

Arnolfo di Cambio (1245–1302) was known as a "crazy reckless" type. His design for the Palazzo Vecchio in Florence (1299–1346) was realized after the Roman intervention and after the reconstruction of the old church of Santa Reparata (now Santa Maria del Fiore). The language he developed was to associate him with both Giotto and Dante: He translated the language of Tuscany into a new and powerful style all his own, neither gothic, romantic, or classical, but truly modern. The Palazzo is the pivotal focus of the city, "radically" imbalanced in design, with an asymmetrical tower and an angular structure. It was to serve as an unambiguous and monumental preface to the work of Brunelleschi.

The architect Brunelleschi was the undisputed master of perspective and space. The interior of his church, Santo Spirito in Florence, pushes the gothic style into the Renaissance.

The vestibule in Michelangelo's Laurentian Library is a tribute to his mannerist tendencies which distort and intellectualize Renaissance tenets.

"The gothic style was created by Suger, abbot of St. Denis, and advisor to two kings of France; the Renaissance, by the merchants of Florence, bankers, and kings of Europe." (N. Pevsner.) Filippo Brunelleschi (1377–1446) was the craftsman of the Renaissance. In the church of Santo Spirito in Florence (1440–65), this inventor of architectural perspective conceived unprecedented mastery of volumetric space.

An architect in spite of himself, Michaelangelo Buonarroti (1475–1564), immersed in the Medici and papal courts, reluctantly accepted the commission of Clement the Seventh to design the Biblioteca Laurenziana (Laurentian Library). By distorting proportions and disrupting "order," he expressed his anger and suspicion of established architectural tenets. The courageous and rebellious invectives of the Laurentian Library (1523–71) make it Michelangelo's true manifesto. The gigantic double columns that bite directly into the wall, and the huge staircase that flows down from the upper level, disrupt the prismatic limitations of the tiny ground entrance. Impervious passages, harsh colors, and syntactic discontinuities all undermine the classicist equilibrium and point the way to the Mannerist style that was to follow. Michelangelo managed to introduce an experience that could only be created by a mind that acknowledged the profanity of death and the unknown of the nonfinite world. Upon entering the space, the visitor is instantly assailed and oppressed, "wishing to escape, feeling like he has participated in a sudden dramatic adventure." (G. de Angelis.) The upper level encloses the library where the oppressive space of the vestibule is contrasted by a structural continuum of architecture and furniture. The rare book room, which was to reconcile the opposing tension of the two spaces, was never built.

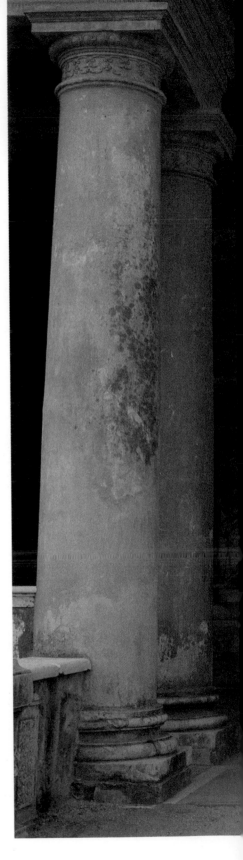

Baldassare
Peruzzi (1481–1536) also questioned
established classical tenets, this
time those of Roman humanism.
His Palazzo Massimo alle Colonne
(1532–36) is known for its surprising
"architecture-within-architecture"
interior, a dazzling intellectual feat
that foreshadowed the baroque era.

An interior shot of
the "room of the gi-
ants" in Giulio Ro-
mano's Palazzo del
Te reveals its fantas-
tic, almost halluci-
natory, frescoes.

The sheer monu-
mentality of Roma-
no's Palazzo del Te
is evident in this
view of the portico.

Despised by nineteenth century puritans be cause of the sensual and aggressive nature of his work, Giulio Pippi, called Giulio Romano (1499–1546), built the Palazzo del Te in Mantova (1525–35) for Federico Gonzaga. It came to be known as the most unprejudiced and disquieting testament to European Mannerism. Romano introduced into the suburban dwelling caustic yet refined innovations: from the multiple facades, to the centralized structures that dispersed within the vast gardens; from the rustic asymmetrical columns of the atrium, to the extraordinary blending of architecture and painting of which the *Caduta dei giganti* ("Decline and Fall of the Giants") is the most famous, he represented a neurotic and disconcerting metaphor for the inevitable decay of the classical ideology.

This anxious search for a new ideology linked Michelangelo and Giulio Romano directly to Andrea Palladio (1508–1580). In the 1570s anti-classicist hyperbole was at its height, inspiring Palladio to refute the rigors of Renaissance rationalism and to confront the idea of a facade as a three-dimensional entity, fully integrated with the internal shape of the building, thereby fusing various volumes in one single architectural plan. The Church of the Redentore (Savior) in Venice (1577–92) reflects this Palladian synthesis. The majestic facade projects a sense of "spaces next to, and yet behind, other spaces" in the interior of the church. (S. Bettini.)

The majestic lyricism of Palladio's Church of the Savior (or *Il Redentore*) graces the shores of the Grand Canal.

The fluid, elastic lines of Borromini's St. Ivo add an extra dimension to the energy of the baroque period.

Francesco Castelli, called Borromini (1599–1667), worked in counterpoint to the baroque Bernini. An anomaly among architects, this problematic introvert was the most successful self-taught artist of sign and construction. Of humble origins, he began his apprenticeship with a stonemason, Carlo Maderna, a relative, and then came under the tutelage of Bernini. In 1634 Borromini went out on his own, and in 1642 began work on the church of S. Ivo alla Sapienza in Rome, which was finished in the 1660s. The surprisingly convex shape of the top level of S. Ivo is based in the curvilinear support of the courtyard and facade. Seven years later, while completing the extraordinary facade of San Carlo alle Quattro Fontane, Borromini committed suicide. His architecture lives and breathes within elastic contours, smooth and calm from a distance, but nervously sculpted and contracted at a close glance.

Not only did modern architect Carlo Scarpa create visionary designs of his own, he was also esteemed for his mastery in architectural restoration. Seen here is his work on Castelvecchio.

The origins of the Carceri d'Invenzioni (Prisons of Invention, 1745–1761), by Giovan Battistta Piranesi (1720–1778), are found in the atria of Roman antiquity. The Carceri express Piranesi's imagination and analysis of the conflicting links between Italy and its past. This same graphic frenzy is shared by two major exponents of modern architecture: the mannerist apostle, Giuseppe Terragni (1904–1943), and the architect-poet, Carlo Scarpa 1906–1978). An artistic zeal that is both exuberant and desperate characterizes the work of Terragni. His Casa del Fascio (Fascist House, 1932–36) in Como is a milestone that shuns rationalist European models. While questioning rationalist assumptions, this structure's "shady perfection" managed to unravel the tenets of a new architectural program in sync with the political changes of the time. Conceived as an open and transparent building where "bureaucracy has no reason to exist," this "glass house" succeeded in moderating the monumentalism and functional purity of the era.

Known for his restoration and restructuring of historic monuments, Scarpa perfected the integration of the modern with an antique, historic environment. Because of his advances, it is no longer possible to merely restore or cheaply imitate former structures. The best example of his ability to converse with the past is the wonderful restoration of Castello Scaligero (1958–68). A great architect-celebrity, Scarpa's regenerative efforts have energized many structures and settings.

Chapter 6

Art

Genova by Sandro Chia, courtesy of Sperone Westwater Gallery

Energy, Dream, and Enigma— Contemporary Italian Art

The post-war generation of Italian painters, sculptors, and printmakers dominates today's international art scene. Theirs is an art which, although not shying from varying degrees of abstraction, is conspicuously figurative and representational. The contemporary Italians have not rejected the imagery and iconography consecrated by the past. Yet, far from retrograde, their art amalgamates, transforms, and reconstructs elements from antiquity, the Renaissance, baroque, expressionist, or metaphysical periods in order to convey a timeless vision. The Italian artists of today do not belong to a single school, nor do they share a unified style. They share, rather, an expansive attitude which embraces the art of the past as a storehouse which may be explored in order to weave new, arresting, and personal fictions. Their images are aesthetically satisfying, mysterious, and open-ended. The new Italian artists are spiritual archeologists, dedicated to unfolding a personal mythology, mirroring their enigmatic inner world. The artwork becomes a revelation of the artist's response to reality, a means of knowing the constructs of the mind which perceives the self and the world.

Bold and uncompromising, Francesco Clemente's untitled color woodblock is a haunting transformation of the face into a mask. (courtesy Martina Hamilton Gallery, New York)

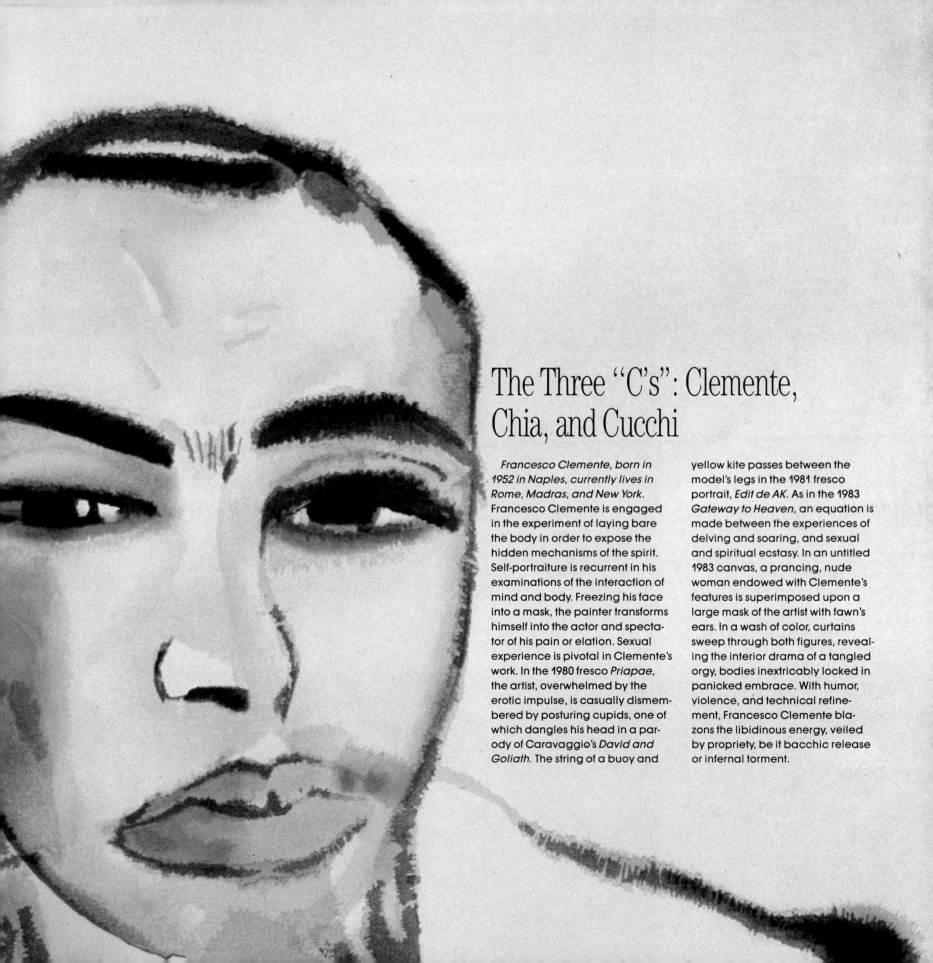

The Three "C's": Clemente, Chia, and Cucchi

Francesco Clemente, born in 1952 in Naples, currently lives in Rome, Madras, and New York. Francesco Clemente is engaged in the experiment of laying bare the body in order to expose the hidden mechanisms of the spirit. Self-portraiture is recurrent in his examinations of the interaction of mind and body. Freezing his face into a mask, the painter transforms himself into the actor and spectator of his pain or elation. Sexual experience is pivotal in Clemente's work. In the 1980 fresco *Priapae,* the artist, overwhelmed by the erotic impulse, is casually dismembered by posturing cupids, one of which dangles his head in a parody of Caravaggio's *David and Goliath.* The string of a buoy and yellow kite passes between the model's legs in the 1981 fresco portrait, *Edit de AK.* As in the 1983 *Gateway to Heaven,* an equation is made between the experiences of delving and soaring, and sexual and spiritual ecstasy. In an untitled 1983 canvas, a prancing, nude woman endowed with Clemente's features is superimposed upon a large mask of the artist with fawn's ears. In a wash of color, curtains sweep through both figures, revealing the interior drama of a tangled orgy, bodies inextricably locked in panicked embrace. With humor, violence, and technical refinement, Francesco Clemente blazons the libidinous energy, veiled by propriety, be it bacchic release or infernal torment.

Enzo *Cucchi, born in 1950 in Ancona, still lives and works there.*

Enzo Cucchi's fantasy is elemental and apocalyptic. The 1982 *Lo Zingaro* ("The Gypsy") is dominated by a raging, flame-red figure. Its arms raised in torment, the figure rushes through a landscape of fire and miasmic accretions of volcanic brown. *La casa vanno in discesa* ("The Houses are Going Downhill") of 1983 evokes a plague-stricken world. Mortality without hope of renewal is suggested by a skull, centered between crumbling, elongated stables. In the distance, an enigmatic horse-drawn carriage races wildly across a vast ocean of fire or blood, streaked with black and dominated by an unclean brown sky. The dashing carriage signals unleashed madness in this geography of tormented self-consciousness. The vast size of the canvas, thirteen by nine feet, suggests the universal devastation of a world given over to dying. A vindictive force assails an earth transformed into hell, a construction of pain. The only possiblity of regeneration is interior, effected through the subjective act of artistic contemplation, comprehending the color and composition of the scene.

Enzo Cucchi's *Lo Zingaro* of 1982 is a powerful depiction of a tortured soul, prey to infernal flames. (courtesy Sperone Westwater Gallery, New York)

Sandro Chia, born in 1946 in Florence, currently lives and works in Rome, Ronciglione, and New York. A new Rubens, Sandro Chia creates large-scale canvases populated by humans inflated to legendary proportions. His is an expansive and effusive art. The magnanimous size of both Chia's work and his personae signals an over-flowing plentitude of life-force. In the manner of the early twentieth century Futurists, Chia's color is rich and molten. His figures are grounded in prismatic harmonies of color, a vibrant magma which pulsates with energy.

A recurrent figure in Chia's painting is the boy or the young man, a visual metaphor for the artist. The youth serves as Chia's double precisely because he possesses an artist's freshness of vision, sensitivity, and openness to experience. Chia's youths most frequently engage in adventures, voyages of exploration. In the 1981 oil on canvas, *The Pharmacist's Son,* a winged Mercury, quicksilver spirit, leads an alchemist's apprentice into a radiant but undefined space. In the 1980 *Genoa,* two light-struck youths levitate, their eyes riveted on a mystery unseen by the viewer of the painting. In the 1980-81, *Very Courageous Boys,* a golden car surrounded by an explosive aureole of confetti—an updated solar chariot—promises a magical adventure in some zone more vibrant than the terrestrial. A raft serves as a conveyance to this realm in the 1983 *Three Boys on a Raft.* As the raft floats on undulations of purple, fawn, and cerulean blue, two monolithic youths wave farewell, flanking a third, of normal proportions, who dreams. Their voyage is a deliverance from the workaday world and a passage toward the unknown. The voyage is Chia's metaphor for the unan-

In Sandro Chia's 1983 *Three Boys on a Raft,* a dreamer flanked by giant guardians drifts into the unknown, unanchored in a sea of prismatic color. (courtesy Sperone Westwater Gallery, New York)

chored spiritual adventure which is artistic creation. The presence of water in this painting is vital both for the translucent coloristic effects it permits the artist and as the element of Helicon, the source of inspiration.

But water also has a threatening aspect in Chia's painting, serving as an element of despair, an infinite abyss which imprisons and separates. In the 1979 *Strange and Gloomy Waters...,* a young girl hurls herself into the still water which mirrors the emptiness of a blue cavern. The 1983 *Lady of the Lake* may be taken as an allegory of the painful aspect of the artist's

severance from society and its material aspirations. An abandoned Ariadne reclines on a narrow rock, against a single, barren tree, gesturing sorrowfully at the murky water which surrounds her.

Yet the solitude given form by Chia's Ariadne is the precondition of self-knowledge and inspiration. The plaint of the *Lady of the Lake* is counterbalanced by affirmative solitude in Chia's work. In the 1983 *Poetic Declaration,* a lone figure set against a flame-toned sky and the liquescent green flame of trees casts forth his utterance to the wind. The poetic declamation effects an essential harmony be-

tween man and nature which Chia also captures in the painted and sculpted versions of *Young Man with Vegetation.* Vegetation and the human form are allied in a paradisiacal state of non-differentiation. Chia's new Adam is rooted in the earth, the tree with its promise of organic growth becoming his very skeleton. The artwork, for Sandro Chia, is a threshold, the entranceway to the Eden of the imagination, a pre-lapsed state of integration of self and universe. The vibrance of Chia's coloration, the magnitude of his figures, serve the artist's affirmation of man's spiritual stature, worth, and dignity.

Mimmo Paladino

Mimmo Paladino's creation invites the viewer into a world of elegant enigma. A stylistic juncture of the Byzantine and the tribal African is evident in the interior drama of *Tre Comete*. (courtesy Sperone Westwater Gallery, New York)

Mimmo Paladino, born in 1948 in Paduli, currently lives and works in Benevento. "Non nasconde forse più misteri il giardino del bosco?": "Is there not perhaps more mystery hidden in the garden than in the forest?" Mimmo Paladino has posited, revealing a central concern of his creation. The garden, collaboration of nature and the human mind, implies a will to artifice. Nature, in effect, becomes resonant with meaning to the extent that it is contained and "cultivated," conforming to human thought and imagination. Not untrammeled freedom but a concentrated and harmonious order is the true source of fascination.

Paladino's is an art of

An Ashanti-style warrior is the messenger to a realm of inwardness and stasis in Paladino's 1982 bronze, *Hortus Conclusis.* The walled garden of the title is the sculptor's metaphor for a harmonious cultivation of nature and for artistic creation as something hidden. (courtesy Sperone Westwater Gallery, New York)

cultivation—linear, lucid, and elegant. He is the heir of the courtly tradition of fifteenth century Siena with its curvilinear, other-worldly forms, as well as of Modigliani's attenuations and elongations. Like Modigliani, Paladino is drawn to the stylizations of African art. But where Modigliani's elongations denote sensuality, physical luxuriance, and ease, Paladino's distortions of the human face and form effect a dematerialization. A scarlet frame surmounted with African masks and a Fuseli-like demon gesturing to ward off the evil eye encompasses an untitled 1983 oil and collage. The frame forms a proscenium arch, revealing a vision of pallid, enthroned spirits, signaling in a swirling mist. In his 1983 oil and collage, *Tre Comete,* three attenuated magicians waver in a scarlet, cubistic space. At once powerful and anonymous, Paladino's disembodied figures are shade-like denizens of the unconscious mind.

African Shamanism and Catholicism are fused in Paladino's visionary art, in which the drama of death and regeneration is a recurring theme. The 1984 etching, *Traglilleiri,* is an arresting example. A border of totemistic animals and crouching men frames an interior image—a nun whose pale face emerges from the darkness of a crypt-like space. To her right, a dark cross dominates the sepia-toned gloom, a sign of regeneration in this realm of shadow. The woman's aristocratic hands, crossed and stigmatized, are more alive than her frozen face. Within her columnar body, she bears a nude being. This inmost, secret spirit or self receives the whispered communication of an animal. It is nurtured by unconsciousness and primeval forces. Paladino's etching suggests the gestation of new, complete selfhood. His still nun is pregnant with spirit or soul.

In the mythology of all peoples, spiritual rebirth is preceded by self-annihilation, a passage through death. This passage is the subject of the 1982 bronze, *Hortus Conclusus.* In this "sealed garden," Paladino equates containment and inwardness, turning from the world to the depths of being, the underworld which lies within. The dominant figure of this sculptural group is an Ashanti warrior, immobile guide of a dark boat. His passenger is a reclining female figure, her radiant patina contrasting with the funereal hue of the vessel. The African warrior, staff aloft, is at once a Hermes leading the luminous spirit to a magic other world of dream, and an Orpheus re-emerging from the depths with the still-slumbering Eurydice, his wife and inspiration. The uncanny thrust of the barge and its uncertain direction suggests both possibilities. The spatial distortion and immobility of *Hortus Conclusus* creates, moreover, a mood of arrested time, a melding of past, present, and future in a suspended world of sculpture. Death, in Paladino's art, is omnipresent but not fearful. The motionlessness of non-being becomes an attribute of beauty, a stilling of life for contemplation.

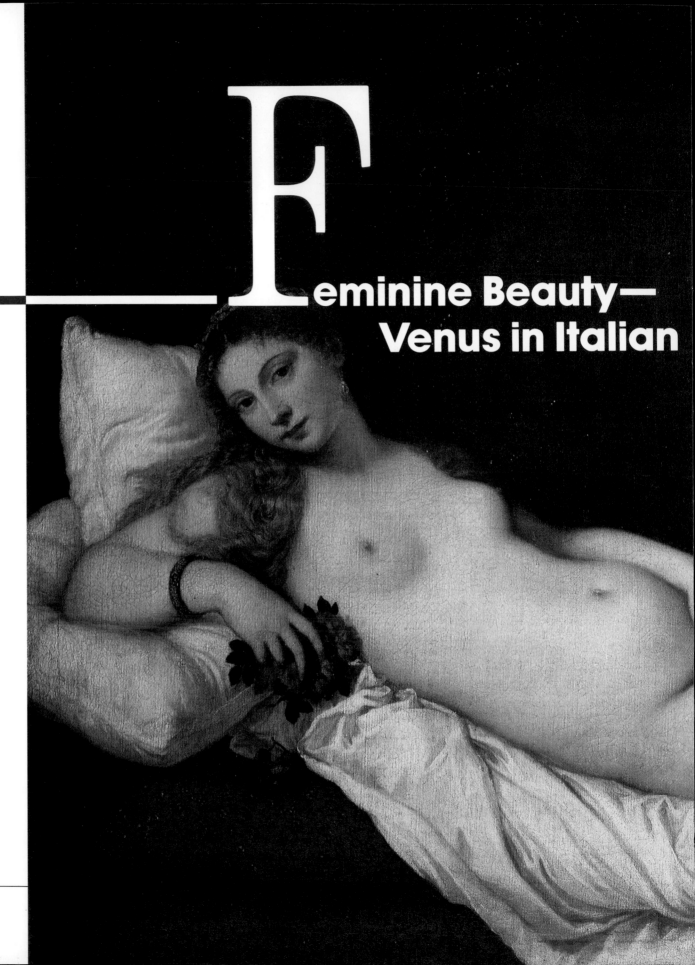

Feminine Beauty— Venus in Italian

The artists of the Italian Renaissance produced indelible images which have long represented the pinnacle of western cultural achievement. In portraiture, mythological, and religious art, the Italian masters captured human experience in all of its multiplicity. Spiritual and physical love were not excluded from their canvases. Indeed, the classical Venus, goddess of love and beauty, inspired masterworks imbued with the Renaissance ideal of harmonious balance and calm. The Venuses created by the Italians have exerted their fascination over the centuries, molding and defining our concepts of grace, beauty, and poise.

In the fifteenth century, the Italians, long masters at depicting the beauty of the Madonna, began also exploring the physical beauty of the nude woman. Depicted as

Renaissance Painting

goddesses of love, the Italian nudes became devotional images in the truest sense; the beauty of these paintings, sumptuous harmonies of line and color, are worthy of admiration and worship.

Perhaps the most famous of the Renaissance goddesses of beauty is the Florentine, Botticelli's *The Birth of Venus,* 1485–90. In a delicately drawn tempera on linen, the goddess floats to earth at Cyprus, her body a pearl born of the sea. She stands naked, pristine, and modest, cloaked in golden coils of hair. Xephyrs cool the young goddess with their gentle breeze, strewing roses in her path. A nymph holds a regal, flower-embroidered robe to clothe the impassive beauty, still new to the world and standing aloof in her idealized perfection.

Contrasting with Botticelli's chaste goddess, a mood of knowing sensuality and languor pervades the Venetian Titian's *Venus of*

Pristine beauty is revealed in Botticelli's vernal *Birth of Venus,* c. 1485-1490.

Urbino, 1538. Set in a luxuriously appointed bedroom, the painting is a rich study in texture and coloration. Passively awaiting her maids, Titian's Venus confronts the viewer, reclining on damask cushions overlaid with snowy linen. In the subdued morning light, the glint of golden jewels relieves the white undulation of her nudity. One hand is lost is a soft mass of rose petals, the other hides her secret charms. A lap dog, connoting fidelity and sensuality, lies curled at her feet. A moment of frank nudity and ease is forever held in Titian's painted dream of desire.

The mannerist, Bronzino, detaches his Venus from the lyricism of Botticelli and Titian. In *Allegory,* 1545, the goddess, strangely elongated and sculptural, at once flesh and cool marble, willingly accepts the lascivious caress of a cupid. On the right, a satyr-like Putto, representing leisure, hurls roses at the lovers. On the left, tormented masks of jealousy and ill-repute writhe. Bronzino suggests that sensuality is never entirely free of painful consequence. Yet, the unashamedly sensual embrace of Venus and the cupid remains the focal image of the allegory, epitomizing the Italians' acceptance of the body and its pleasures.

Physical exuberance motivates Annibale Carracci's *Venus, a Satyr, and Two Cupids* of 1588. Sprawling on russet silk in an autumnal grove, a statuesque Venus displays her abundant flesh to the viewer. She embodies the fullness of the harvest season. A leering satyr offers Venus a chalice shimmering with green and purple grapes, a brimming cup of intoxication. One attendant cupid teases the satyr and the other grasps Venus's leg, licking his lips in a mischievous gesture of appetite. Carracci's scene is frolicsome, expressive of joy and celebration.

Annibale Carracci created a lascivious paean to intoxication in his 1588 *Venus, a Satyr, and Two Cupids.*

Chapter 7

Literature and Film

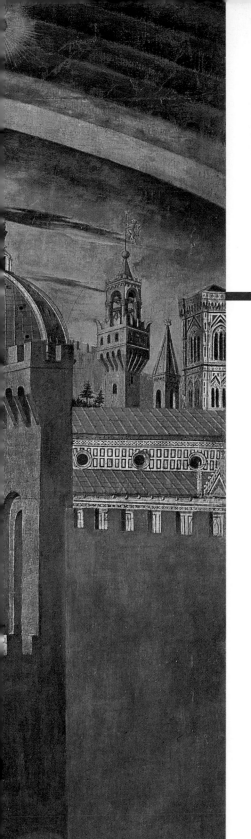

The Florentines—Dante, Petrarch, and Boccaccio

This portrait of Dante painted by de Michelino shows the poet with his masterpiece, *The Divine Comedy*. The Duomo of Florence, Dante's native city, rises on his right. To Dante's left is an allegory representing his vision of the Inferno, behind him are Purgatory and Paradise.

Italy's literary tradition is one of the richest and most rewarding in the world. Since the late Middle Ages, Italians have been masters of narrative and poetic image. Foremost is Dante Alighieri (1265–1321), the first writer to compose in Italian, the language of the people, rather than in Latin, the favored language of the learned. Dante's masterwork is *The Divine Comedy*, a tripartite epic poem which projects the soul's fate after death. In *The Inferno*, Dante, guided by the Roman poet, Virgil, interrogates the damned. The prisoners of hell, many of whom are Dante's adversaries, or friends, relate their personal stories of lost illusion, vice, betrayal, and political folly. Dante's is a teeming hell, crowded with lost souls locked in a claustrophobic community of despair. Yet, each soul is alone in its pain, forever cut off from God's pardon. In the second book of the *Comedy*, the *Purgatorio*, Dante leaves hell and begins a slow, expiatory ascension toward heaven. In the *Paradiso*, he is vouchsafed a vision of divine radiance, led by Beatrice, the angelic woman who personifies transcendent purity and grace.

Francesco Petrarch is famed for developing the sonnet, the brief, fourteen-line form capable of enclosing an entire world of individual experience. In his collection of poems, the *Canzoniere*, Petrarch celebrates his unrequited love for Laura, ideal woman and muse. Using imagery of storm, fever, and shipwreck, Petrarch sings his nostalgia for Laura's unattainable beauty in verse which is as fresh and moving today as at the time of its composition.

Less rarified is the writing of Boccaccio (1313–1375), who explores the pleasures of physical love in his collection of ribald tales, the *Decameron*. These proto-short stories are the narratives of a group of well-born travellers who have escaped the plague in Florence and sought shelter in a country villa. Powerful realism, psychological intuition, farce, and street language blend in Boccaccio's prose. The themes of the *Decameron* are various, ranging from knightly adventures with happy endings to tragedies, from love intrigues to cruel jokes and licentious experience. The *Decameron* mirrors the entire world of the early Renaissance, its honest passion, humor, moral complexities, and aspirations.

DOMINVS IOHANNES BOCCACCIVS

The Decameron, Boccaccio's masterpiece, contains a variety of themes, from adventures with happy endings, ribald tales, cruel hoaxes, and love stories, to clever intrigues and vulgar, lusty, licentious experiences (afterwards called *boccacesche*). His portrait here is painted by the Renaissance master, Andrea del Castagno.

While Dante was inspired by Beatrice, Petrarch, shown here in a sixteenth-century portrait, had Laura for his muse. Petrarch created some of the world's most beautiful poetry in her name.

Today's Writers

Dino Buzzati

Although not yet widely read outside of Italy, Buzzati is acclaimed in Europe for his dream-like style and distortion of time. Novelist, playwright, painter, art critic, and cartoonist, Buzzati examines ordinary events and discloses terror concealed by the veil of normalcy. The real and the unreal, the dramatic and poetic combine in Buzzati's works, *Il Desert dei Tartari* (1940), *I Sette Messaggeri* (1942), and *Paura alla Scala* (1948).

C. E. Gadda

His vision grotesque and ironic, Gadda is considered by Italians to be their most revolutionary writer. Influenced by Joyce's neologisms and stream-of-consciousness style, Gadda has experimented with distortions of language, creating mixtures of Milanese and Roman dialect which strike even the Italian ear as esoteric.

Alberto Moravia

Unlike Gadda's, Moravia's style is straightforward and accessible. His writing, like Boccaccio's, is frank and explicit. Treatment of sex is used as a tool of provocation, an incisive means of exploding conformism, hypocrisy, and self-righteous morality. His most popular novels have been translated into English. Among them are *Agostino* (1944), *The Conformist* (1951), and *Boredom* (1960).

Italo Calvino

Recently deceased, Calvino is an acclaimed writer of philosophical and metaphysical tales which examine man's relation to the universe in a serio-comic manner. Works such as *The Cloven Viscount, The Castle of Crossed Destinies,* and *If on a Winter's Night, A Traveller...* share in the nature of the fable and folk tale, emphasizing the magical and miraculous in the midst of the everyday. Calvino is a worthy successor of the Renaissance storyteller. He is a master of allegory and fantasy, with a lucid voice and succinct style uniquely his own.

Umberto Eco

A scholar, writer, and essayist, Umberto Eco has achieved worldwide fame for his thriller set in the Middle Ages, *The Name of the Rose.* The novel may be read on several levels — as a detective story, as a discourse on medieval philosophy, or as an exercise in semiotics (that is, as a group of clues hidden in the very language of the text). At once dense and entertaining, this provocative novel, set in a medieval abbey, has been read both for pleasure and instruction.

Among other great contemporary writers, Cesare Pavese must be mentioned for his probing examinations of loneliness and boredom. With a style all the more forceful and disconcerting for its spareness, Pavese dissects the lives of representative members of all of Italy's social classes. Giuseppe Lampedusa, on the other hand, has concentrated on the vanishing world of the aristocracy. *The Leopard* details the reactions of a princely Sicilian family to the advent of Garibaldi and the democratization of Italy.

Primo Levi has written novels about Jewish persecution in fascist Italy. Leonardo Sciascia has convincingly chronicled the world of the Sicilian Mafia. Pier Paolo Pasolini, Marxist writer, poet, man of the theater and film, scandalized the public with his investigations of violence and the life of the slums. Elsa Morante has delved the female psyche as revealed in love relationships played against a backdrop of war and revolutionary change. It is clear from this brief survey that Italian literature today offers a variety of styles and themes, all of which express concern for humanity and its adjustment to a difficult and uncertain century.

Novelist, journalist, and film critic, Alberto Moravia is probably the best known contemporary Italian writer outside of Italy.

Italian Film

Roberto Rossellini

The great American director, Otto Preminger, once remarked that film history could be devided into two phases, before and after *Roma Città Aperta* by Roberto Rossellini. Rossellini is the father of Italian neorealism. In *Rome, Open City* (1945) and *Paisa* (1946), he confronted the harsh circumstances of post-war

Ingrid Bergman created a scandal when she left her husband and child for the great film director Roberto Rossellini. They fell in love while filming a movie together and were married some time later.

Italy. Rossellini believed that the director must remain outside of his film, an objective observer and narrator of events rather than an interpreter or commentator.

After three early films concerned with the aftermath of World War II and the plight of society as a whole, Rossellini turned to individual experience. This shift in focus is evident in *Stromboli Terra di Dio*, a love story starring the radiant Ingrid Bergman, who later became Rossellini's wife. The director became increasingly interested in historical rather than contemporary events. By approaching a subject distant in time, Rossellini hoped to gain objectivity in his portrayal of human life. He was drawn to the great, filming *The Acts of the Apostles* (1968), *Socrates* (1970), *Pascal* (1972), and *DesCartes* (1974). Many of his biographical films were conceived for television, establishing a tradition of quality in the Italian mass media.

Luchino Visconti

Scion of a Milanese aristocratic family, Luchino Visconti turned to filmmaking late in life, after first establishing a career as a set designer and stage director. The visual understanding which he cultivated for the stage carries over into his films, which are opulent, and richly detailed and composed. Like Rossellini, Visconti's first film efforts were marked by strict realism. *La Terra Trema* [1948] confronts the post-war exploitation of the poor by the wealthy classes. Three years later, he filmed *Bellissima*, starring the powerful Anna Magnani as a frustrated lower-class mother coarsened by poverty, yet harboring impossible dreams for the daughter whom she tyrannizes. This complex interpersonal relationship would find echoes in Visconti's later films, which deal with individual frustration and anxiety played against a vividly drawn backdrop of decadence. Many of Visconti's films are specifically literary in inspiration or mood. *The Leopard* (1963), based on Lampedusa's novel, depicts the lifestyle of a noble Sicilian family at the moment that they lose power. In *The Damned* (1969), Visconti again focuses on a family, this time of corrupt industrialists in Nazi Germany, whose ruthlessness and depravity parallel political events. In 1971, Visconti filmed Thomas Mann's *Death in Venice*, a symbolic story of an obsessive love which leads to death. Visconti's attention to costumes and the scenic details of a resort hotel on the Lido allow the viewer entrance into a world of fin-de-siecle luxury. *Ludwig* (1972) studies the insanity of the king of Bavaria who sponsored Richard Wagner. *The Innocent* (1974), Visconti's final film, is based on the novel by Gabriele D'Annunzio. Also set at the turn of the century, *The Innocent* conjures the fury of a jaded and amoral nobleman who murders the baby born of his wife's infidelity. As in all of Visconti's films, *The Innocent* is unsurpassed for its refined and meticulous recreation of a particular ambience. The pampered ease which surrounds Visconti's characters frees them from the struggle for existence. Their anxiety turns inward. The final films are documents of destructive passion and self-destructiveness.

Anouk Aimee and Marcello Mastroianni pick up a prostitute and cruise the streets of Rome in one of the greatest films ever made, Fellini's *La Dolce Vita*.

Donald Sutherland as Casanova is caught in yet another amorous adventure. Fellini's film of the same name had a surreal, dream-like quality to it.

The maestro himself, Federico Fellini, talking with an actor on the set.

Federico Fellini

Felliniesque has become an adjective for the mixture of the magic, grotesque, and nostalgic which characterizes this great master's films. Rich in symbols and metaphors, Fellini's movies present life as an ever-shifting carnival, evoked in a vivid montage of faces and places. Nothing is excluded from the panoply of his films, populated by priests, nuns, prostitutes, the poor, the aristocracy, fascists, clowns, dwarfs, children, and the elderly. *I Vitelloni* examines the life of clowns wandering the provinces. *La Strada* is a vision of man's desperate solitude, as is *La Dolce Vita*, the chronicle of a journalist's voyage through the corrupt world of the Roman demi-monde. After *La Dolce Vita*, Fellini's films became more fantastic in their mood of unreality and more elaborate in surreal visual detail. The ancient Rome of his *Satyricon* is a timeless world of decadence, as is the stylized Venice of *Casanova*. In *Roma*, the eternal city is brought to the brink of apocalypse, while in *Amarcord*, Fellini's provincial childhood is recreated. Fellini's most recent film is *Ginger & Fred*, a genial director's bow to the greats of the cinematic past and an attack on the medium of television.

Chapter 8

Music and Theater

Italian Comedy— From the Commedia dell'Arte to Dario Fo

The Commedia dell'Arte

Since the sixteenth century, Arlecchino—or Harlequin—has been the King of Jesters. In this advertisement, a traditional Harlequin in motley triumphantly towers above a bustling circus.

The Italians have long been renowned for their comic gift, their ease of gesticulation, mimicry, and clever comeback. Their reputation for comic genius was founded as far back as the mid-sixteenth century. Between the years 1550 and 1750, the Italians dominated the international comic theater with performances by the strolling players, the *commedia dell'arte.* The rage of Europe for two hundred years, the Italian "commedia" was originally developed by professional actors in rejection of the scholarly Latin theater practiced by the dilettantes of the Renaissance courts. Unlike the dilettantes, these commedia actors were highly trained and multi-talented; hence *dell'arte,* artful. The Italian comedians enlivened the stage with movement. Their performances were a total spectacle, involving virtuoso musicianship, skilled dancing, and outrageous acrobatics — catapulting handsprings and clowning contortions. The commedia was popular, improvised theater, requiring quick wit and easy interaction from the actors. The métier of the Italian comedian was much different from that of the traditional actor who recites lines. Playwrights and finished scripts were never employed. Action and dialogue were instead invented and improvised by the resourceful actors in the course of the performance. Basic love intrigues were embroidered with timely satire, the scandal of the moment, and with the actor's *lazzi,* scurrilous and often obscene comic turns. Appealing in its forthright directness and energy to every level of society, the commedia was frequently mildly subversive, with comic servants, the *zanni,* scheming to outwit their aristocratic or bourgeois masters, often doddering lechers or misers. The carnival spirit, with its intrigue, vibrant colors, and frenetic motion governed the commedia dell'arte.

The commedia actor, like the carnival participant, is a master of disguise and self-transformation. By basic definition, the actor strives in the course of performance to become another. The Italian commedia was also known as the "comedy of masks," since its actors wore characteristic disguises, playing the same fixed type again and again. Of the stereotyped servants, masters, and young lovers which comprised a commedia troupe, only the lovers, the most beautiful and youthful members of the company, were unmasked. The others participated in a gaudy masquerade, wearing costumes which exaggerated and underlined the distinctive personalities of their character. The costume and mask permitted the character always to be the same, often grotesque, type, regardless of the action of the play.

Arlecchino, or Harlequin, is perhaps the best known participant in the commedia masquerade. He was an agile but foolish servant from Bergamo, wearing a patchwork costume, stylized rags, and a black half-mask with a snub nose. The supple Arlecchino could imitate a cat cleaning itself or turn successive backward somersaults without upsetting a glass of wine. He was also adept at scaling walls to reach his beloved Columbina, a flirtatious and lively servant also dressed in patchwork.

Pulcinella (from *pulcino,* "chicken") was second in popularity to Arlecchino. Dressed in a white tunic, sporting a phallic nose and phallic hat, the squawking Pulcinella was a master of disguise, assuming the roles of doctor, servant, or peasant. He was frequent-

ly surrounded by his "little ones," the similarly dressed *pulcinelli.*

Another native of Bergamo, the character of Brighella was a cunning valet, involved in thieving and illicit love. Brighella wore a green costume and bilious green mask, animal-like in expression, a sign of his wily and envious disposition. Pedrolino (or Pierotto or Pierrot) was a foil for Brighella. He was a mute, moonstruck servant dressed in loose white garb with a powdered face. Pedrolino habitually suffered

from unrequited love, a trait he shared with Mezzotino. The latter was a finely dressed servant in red stripes, the most gifted musician in the commedia troupe, who often poured forth his longing in song.

Of the masters, the Captain was a boastful but cowardly Spaniard. Signor Pantalone, merchant of Venice, was an old cuckold and lecher. A leathery brown mask defined his aged face. He was dressed in red with a moneybag dangling over his genitals. His

passion was both unsuitable to his age and expensive to maintain. Pantalone often had recourse to Ruffiana, a witch-like old go-between. Like Pantalone, the Dottore, a physician or lawyer from Bologna, was an old lecher whose amorous exploits ended without success. Spouting a bizarre mixture of pidgin Latin and Bolognese dialect, the Dottore was an obese, waddling figure with a half-mask revealing rouged and flaccid cheeks. Pantalone or the Dottore

frequently had beautiful young daughters, Flaminia, Isabella, or Zerbinetta. Skilled singers and ballerinas, these beauties were magnificently dressed and unmasked, displayed to full advantage. Chaste and refined, these ingénues were the object of the devoted attentions of a youthful Leandro. Both the girls and their suitors expressed their love in elaborate and high-flown language, contrasting with the crass antics of the other players.

Winter in Venice is marked by carnival festivities and masquerade. The bizarre, comic, and sublime commingle in this unforgettable spectacle set in the world's most theatrical city.

Carlo Goldoni

The actors of the Italian commedia emerge as a closely knit and well-loved family, travelling across Europe in groups of twelve and playing wherever an appreciative audience could be found, be it in a palace or in an open-air stall. The wild, unbridled farce of the commedia dell'arte, the spontaneity and directness of an improvisational theater, has never ceased to exert its fascination. The commedia dell'arte did not die, but was transformed by the Venetian playwright, Carlo Goldoni (1707-1793). He used the lovers, buffoons, and lechers of the Italian commedia to expose life as a vast carnival. For Goldoni, the masquerade was no longer a physical reality, but a metaphor for the ruse and chicanery of social posturing. In his written comedies, Goldoni set about to depict the false pretenses imposed by life in a structured society. His model was eighteenth century Venice, the carnival city par excellence, where the entire gentry went about in disguise, enjoying the anonymity and freedom conferred by a half-mask and a voluminous cape. Venice was the perfect manifestation of a society in which everyone indulges in an invisible charade.

In 1747, Goldoni provided a commedia dell'arte troupe with its first written play, *The Clever Woman*, establishing a pattern for his future creations. In the best of his plays (two hundred were written between 1748 and 1767), Goldoni's focal character is a capable and independent woman besieged with suitors. She must choose from a constellation of types, orchestrating her future happiness. Rosaura, in the 1747 *Venetian Twins*, is the object of the attentions of a daring and a timid twin, both played unmasked by a famous Pantalone, Cesare D'Alba. In the 1748 *The Wily Widow*, a beautiful woman assumes various disguises to test the fidelity of her foreign admirers. A result of her research: "Every country is as good as another if you have a full purse and a lively heart." Mirandolina, the innkeeper of the 1753 *La Locandiera*, fends off her amorous guests and tricks a misogynic aristocrat into declaring his love for her. A true Columbina, the vivacious innkeeper then marries a harlequin-like valet. Love might not pay the bills, but the already prosperous Mirandolina finds happiness with someone of her own station. These commedia types were preserved, but placed in the new light of Goldoni's contemporary society. "In order to bring out a character, I have always felt it necessary to contrast it with another character with an opposite nature," Goldoni wrote. His plays, although rooted in the milieu of eighteenth century Venice, are timeless studies of human interaction, type played off against type, the whole recorded with brilliance and *sprezzatura*.

Luigi Pirandello

The spirit of the commedia masquerade is also found in Nobel-Prize winner Luigi Pirandello's (1867-1936) black comedies. For this twentieth century innovator, born in Sicily, the masquerade is no longer a metaphor for life in society, but a matter of philosophical inquiry into the nature of appearance and reality. His major plays are united in the volume, *Maschere Nude (Nude Masks)*. Implicit is the idea that life itself is a theatrical masquerade precisely because it is steeped in illusion. In the early play, *Cosi é se ve ne pare, (It Is, If It Seems So*, 1917), Pirandello reveals a simple plot. Nosy townspeople observe the enigmatic behavior of two newcomers, a man and his mother-in-law, both of whom claim that the other is mad. The author posits: "What can we ever really know about others?" Knowledge about others and about self is impossible since we are all frozen masks defined by the concepts that others form of us.

Enrico IV (1922) depicts the lucid madness of an Italian nobleman who is struck on the head with a rock while masquerading as the eleventh century king, Henry IV. Coming to in a state of madness, he never frees himself from the disguise, forcing others to conform to his fantasy of medieval existence. In the spirit of *Cosi é se ve ne pare*, Enrico becomes what he seems to be. The role of kingship has taken over the masquerader's face. In the renowned *Sei personagi in cerca d'autore*, (*Six Characters in Search of an Author*, 1922), a troupe of actors and a troupe of characters enter into conflict. In the manner of the commedia, the "characters" are fixed types, the mother, the father, the stepdaughter, all eager to instruct the actors in performing their tragic family life. For the characters, the purpose of the theater is to give them life on stage. Yet, they cannot agree on an interpretation of the events of their existence. Each character improvises the drama from his point of view. They come to the realization that true identity is impossible; we are only images for others, masks molded by the roles which we play.

Margaret Courtney-Clarke

The consummate actor, writer, and director, Dario Fo, stands in intense concentration, perhaps ready to begin one of the comic transformations for which he is renowned.

Ornately carved Italian puppets are singularly expressive, mysterious, and regal in this display.

Dario Fo

Disillusionment with life in society also marks contemporary actor-director-playwright Dario Fo's comic theater. Remote from Pirandello's metaphysical speculations, Dario Fo has returned to the original farcical, bawdy spirit of the commedia dell'arte. Like Goldoni, Fo wishes us to understand ourselves in terms of contemporary society, thereby enabling us to emerge from societal stereotypes. Although Marxist theater and humor would seem, at first glance, incompatible, Fo's comedy of provocation is indeed rollicking, based on mistaken identities, multiple identities, earthy language, and knock-out antics. Like the strolling players of the Renaissance, enacting the triumph of wily servants over greedy masters, Fo is convinced that humor is the best means to define the social inequities which he finds rampant in the capitalist West. Such plays as *The Accidental Death of an Anarchist* and *We Won't Pay, We Won't Pay* share in the improvisational spirit of the commedia. They were written in response to specific events and the texts are apt to vary between performances. Like the commedia dell'arte, Fo's political theater demands versatility of the actor, who becomes clown, acrobat, and oracle of freedom.

MUSIC AND THEATER

Opera: Rossini, Verdi, and Pavarotti

Gioachino Rossini (1792–1868)

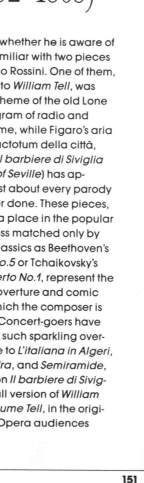

This portrait of Rossini shows a voracious, spirited man, qualities often found in his comedic operas. The undisputed master of the *opera buffa*, Rossini was equally at home with serious opera.

Everyone, whether he is aware of it or not, is familiar with two pieces by Gioachino Rossini. One of them, the overture to *William Tell*, was used as the theme of the old Lone Ranger program of radio and television fame, while Figaro's aria "Largo a il factotum della città, largo" from *Il barbiere di Siviglia* (*The Barber of Seville*) has appeared in just about every parody of opera ever done. These pieces, which have a place in the popular consciousness matched only by such other classics as Beethoven's *Symphony No.5* or Tchaikovsky's *Piano Concerto No.1*, represent the two genres, overture and comic opera, for which the composer is best known. Concert-goers have long adored such sparkling overtures as those to *L'italiana in Algeri*, *La gazza ladra*, and *Semiramide*, not to mention *Il barbiere di Siviglia* and the full version of *William Tell* (or *Guillaume Tell*, in the original French). Opera audiences

151

Margaret Courtney-Clarke

have similarly delighted to the whole of *Il barbiere*, as well as *L'italiana in Algeri* and *La Cenerentola* (*Cinderella*). No one who has heard them can forget such numbers as the hilarious quintet "Va sassopra il mio cervello" from *L'italiana*, with its nonsense syllables "cra cra, bum bum, din din, tac tac," or the equally amusing sextet "Questo è un nodo avviluppato" from *La Cenerentola*.

But overture and comic opera are only part of the story. Rossini's contemporaries admired him above all as a composer of serious opera, the genre which represents the overwhelming majority of his work. From his first major success at the age of twenty-one, with *Tancredi*, to his premature retirement just sixteen years later, after *Guillaume Tell*, serious opera was the order of the day. These works are not mere historical curiosities, but masterpieces every bit as stage-worthy as their more celebrated comic siblings. Audiences are now rediscovering the power and beauty of such works as *Otello, Mosè in Egitto, Maometto II,* and *Semiramide*, and have begun to appreciate why, in the words of musicologist Philip Gossett, "No composer in the first half of the nineteenth century enjoyed the measure of prestige, wealth, popular acclaim, or artistic influence that belonged to Rossini. His contemporaries recognized him as the greatest Italian composer of his time." Indeed, along with this re-evaluation of Rossini's serious operas, it can be said without exaggeration that such things as the initiation of a new critical edition of all his works and the institution of a summer festival in his home town of Pesaro represent a veritable "Rossini Renaissance."

A debut in the La Scala opera house is a triumph for opera singers and an event for an appreciative audience. Located in Milan, La Scala has been home to many of the greatest singers of our time.

Margaret Courtney-Clarke

Giuseppe Verdi (1813–1901)

Like that of no other composer, the career of Giuseppe Verdi is linked to the history of his country. The Risorgimento, the period in which Italy freed itself of foreign domination and became a united, independent nation, coincides with the first half of his life, and its influence on him was profound. As the twentieth century composer Luigi Dallapiccola wrote, "The phenomenon that is Verdi is unimaginable without the Risorgimento. Whether or not he played an active part in it is unimportant: he absorbed its air and its tone… [and] formulated a style through which the Italian people found a key to their dramatic plight and vibrated in unison with it." Even his name became part of a patriotic cry, with "Viva Verdi!" at once a celebration of the composer and of Vittorio Emanuele, Re D'Italia—Victor Emanuel II, the first king of unified Italy. Such was Verdi's popularity with his countrymen that in 1861 he became an honorary deputy in Italy's first Parliament.

Unlike Rossini, Verdi composed operas all his adult life, in a career that spanned some sixty years. His mature output, which began in 1842, is usually divided into four periods. The first of these, which runs until 1849, is the least known to modern audiences. Not so with the Italian public of the time, which flocked to such works as *Nabucco, I lombardi alla prima crociata, Attila,* and *La battaglia di Legnano.* Revolutionary Italians readily identified with such moments as the chorus of Hebrew exiles "Va pensiero, sull'ali dorate" from *Nabucco,* which even today is a sort of unofficial Italian national anthem. In a more general sense, as the critic Andrew Porter writes, "beyond any specific 'relevance,' there was and is [in these operas] the power of Verdi's melodies and strong, slow-surging rhythms to generate mass emotion." Today, audiences are rediscovering these and other operas, such as *Ernani* and *Macbeth.* Like Rossini's serious operas, the operas of Verdi's first maturity are coming to take their rightful place in the repertory.

Verdi's second period, which runs from 1849 to 1853, contains some of the most popular operas ever written. *Luisa Miller, Rigoletto, Il Trovatore,* and *La Traviata* are in a sense the antithesis of the early operas. On a more personal, intimate level, they explore the complexities of human emotions without eschewing the expressive power in the works of the first period.

With this second period ended what Verdi called his "years in the galley." Having averaged more than one opera a year for over ten years, he had now achieved the wealth and fame that allowed him to choose his projects as he pleased.

From 1855 to 1871, he produced just six operas, *Les vêpres siciliennes, (I Vespri Siciliani), Simon Boccanegra, Un Ballo in Maschera, La Forza del destino, Don Carlos,* and *Aida,* plus a major revision of *Macbeth.* All of them are more or less influenced by French grand opera — indeed, *Les vêpres* and *Don Carlos,* written for the Paris Opera, have French libretti. In them, monumental stage effects alternate with moments of the most delicate lyricism.

After *Aida,* Verdi entered a long period of semi-retirement. Besides the *Requiem,* a revised Italian version of *Don Carlos,* and an important revision of *Simon Boccanegra,* he produced nothing important until *Otello* (1887) and *Falstaff* (1893), his last two operas. Arguably the finest Italian operas of the nineteenth century, they represent a lifetime of experience in musical dramaturgy. Drawn from Shakespeare, they are the worthy farewell of an unsurpassed master.

Luchiano Pavarotti (1935-   )

As if fate had decreed it, Luciano Pavarotti was born in Modena, a small provincial capital in Italy's Po Valley halfway between Verdi's Busseto and Rossini's boyhood home of Bologna. One of the finest and most celebrated tenors of his generation, he has given outstanding performances of the music of both these masters.

The son of a baker who is also a fine amateur tenor, Pavarotti was exposed to music at an early age. Remembering his father, he has written, "He would bring home records of all the great tenors of the day—Gigli, Martinelli, Schipa, Caruso—and would play them over and over. Hearing those great voices all the time, it was inevitable that I would try to sing like that, too."

Yet despite his early interest in singing and his involvement in the local church choir, Pavarotti did not seriously consider a singing career until his early twenties. It was then that he began studying voice in earnest, supporting himself first by teaching elementary school and later by selling insurance. He made rapid progress. As the tenor Arrigo Pola, one of his voice teachers, recalls, "If I would tell him something or demonstrate a way of producing a tone, he would pick it up right away. It was not tiring to teach Luciano: He got things so quickly.... From the start, I never doubted Luciano would one day be a very great tenor."

After winning an important competition in 1961, Pavarotti made his professional operatic debut on April 28 of that year as Rodolfo in Puccini's *La Bohème* at the Teatro Municipale in nearby Reggio Emilia. Shortly thereafter, in another nearby town, Carpi, he gave his first performance in the part of the Duke of Mantua in Verdi's *Rigoletto*. Both of these roles are among his favorites, and both of them were featured, along with Alfredo in Verdi's *La Traviata*, in his first season at Milan's La Scala in 1965-66.

Before his success at La Scala, however, Pavarotti spent several years singing abroad. As he writes, "Italians are skeptical of anything native, particularly tenors. On the other hand, anything foreign wins quick respect whether it is toothpaste or singers. It is sad that so many Italian singers must go abroad to achieve their success and are passed over in their own country." One of the decisive influences in the years before La Scala was his work with the soprano Joan Sutherland, with whom he toured Australia in the spring of 1965. Writes Pavarotti, "She showed me a number of exercises that would strengthen the key muscles. I worked very hard at them. I also watched her constantly, often putting my hands on her rib cage to feel what was happening when she sang. When I finished the tour my diaphragm was much stronger, my use of it more automatic, and my vocal chords were in far better physical shape."

Pavarotti's New York Metropolitan Opera debut came in November of 1968. Once again, he was featured in the role of Rodolfo in *La Bohème*. Despite a bout of influenza, he was described by Peter G. Davis in *The New York Times* as follows: "Mr. Pavarotti triumphed principally through the natural beauty of his voice—a bright, open instrument with a nice metal-

lic ping up top that warms into an even, burnished luster in mid-range. Any tenor who can toss off high C's with such abandon, successfully negotiate delicate diminuendo effects, and attack Puccinian phrases so fervently is going to win over any *La Bohème* audience, and Pavarotti had them eating out of his hand."

But Pavarotti's real Metropolitan success, the one which catapulted him to international fame, came some three years later, in February of 1972. After appearing as Tonio in Donizetti's *La fille du régiment* along with Joan Sutherland, he became that rarest of rarities, an opera singer known not just to specialists and opera fans, but to people with no special interest in opera as well. With appearances on television talk shows and cover articles in leading news magazines, Luciano Pavarotti can truly be called a superstar.

Pavarotti's voice distinguishes itself by a number of exceptional qualities. Besides its beautiful tone and the effortless clarity of its high notes, it is remarkably even throughout its range. In addition,

Pavarotti brings to it his own gifts as an interpreter, with sensitive phrasing and clear pronunciation. Indeed, for all his notoriety as the "King of the High C's," he puts much more emphasis on diction and phrasing. "Good enunciation should be worked on and worked on—slaved over, really—until it becomes automatic," he writes, and "to make so much of the high C is silly. Caruso didn't have it. Neither did Tito Schipa. As a matter of fact, Schipa didn't even have a great voice, but he was a great singer. He had a great line. For producing music, that is ten times more important."

Pavarotti's repertory consists for the most part of music by Bellini, Donizetti, Verdi, and Puccini. Although he has never sung in a live production of any opera by Rossini, his recording of Arnoldo in an Italian-language version of *Guillaume Tell* is outstanding. As for Verdi, his favorite roles are the Duke in *Rigoletto* and Riccardo in *Un Ballo in Maschera*. To all his roles, he brings unerring musical instinct and the magic of a unique voice.

Pavarotti's rich and resonant voice has distinguished him as one of the greatest tenors of his generation. He has also been credited with bringing opera to people who had never before been exposed to classical singing.

Chapter 9

Invention and Sport

The Inventive Italians

A Glaser poster commemorating the ever-popular, bright red Olivetti Valentine typewriter.

In Padua, in the year 1348, Giovanni Dondi completed construction of the first astronomical clock, capable of accurately recording not only the movements of five planets, but also keeping a calendar of church feasts. We may take Dondi's clock as an emblem of the Italian genius, which embraces both speculative thought and practical application. Through both speculation and invention, Italian scientists have changed our conception of the universe and improved our way of life.

Motivated by an unquenchable thirst for knowledge of the visible world, the painter, Leonardo da Vinci (1452-1519), was the greatest theoretician of the Renaissance. As a geologist, Leonardo studied the formation of fossils and mountain ranges, the latter serving as a recurrent background in his paintings. Leonardo's keen observation served experiments in optics, hydraulics, and anatomy. He designed bridges and canals, and also speculated on the construction of ballistic missiles, flying machines, and parachutes. Fascinated by the potential of automation to save time and labor, the painter's notebooks contain myriad drawings of machines and cogs which would only be realized centuries later.

The modern age was heralded by the Italian physicist and astronomer, Galileo Galilei (1564-1642), who braved the bigotry of the Inquisition in order to diffuse his observations of the solar system. At the age of nineteen, in 1583, while still a student at the University of Pisa, Galileo made the first of his famous studies of gravitational pull. He noted that distance, rather than the weight of an object, determined the speed of its fall. In 1592, while a professor of mathematics in Padua, Galileo studied parabolic movement, inertia, and the mechanism of sound frequency. Moving to Venice in the first decade of the seventeenth century, the peripatetic scientist supervised the grinding of magnifying lenses and began the first experiments in telescopy. He observed the surface of the moon, the Milky Way, the rotation of the sun on its axis, and the phases of Venus—all of which substantiated the Copernican theory that the planets revolve around the sun. In 1616, Galileo was denounced and warned by the Inquisition not to teach this heretical view of the solar system. Nonetheless, in 1632, the undaunted Galileo published a dialogue, "Dialogo sopra i due massimi sistemi del mondo," defending the idea of orbit around the sun. He was summoned before Pope Urban VIII in 1633 and exiled to Siena. Blind but unvanquished, Galileo continued to receive disciples, instructing them in the laws of physics which he had defended and discovered. His last book, written in 1638, *Concerning Two New Sciences*, a definitive summation of his life's work in physics and astronomy, is considered a monument of Western scientific thought.

The revolutionary changes inaugurated by Galileo in the seventeenth century have parallels in the discoveries of two twentieth century Nobel Prize winners. Guglielmo Marconi (1874-1937) was a pioneer of wireless telegraphy. At the age of twenty-one, while a student at the University of Bologna, Marconi constructed the first successful wireless apparatus, initiating the epoch of instantaneous communication. In 1897, he moved to England and established communication over a distance of nine miles. By 1899, he could send signals across the Atlantic. Wireless telegraphy was soon used to rescue ships in distress. By 1914, Marconi established the first

and—highly lucrative—
radiotelephonic service. During
World War I, he experimented with
short waves and, before his death,
had conceived of television. It was
Marconi who changed our mode
of communication, conquering
distance with sound, facilitating
rapid exchange of information,
transforming our globe into a
global village.

Enrico Fermi (1901-1954) is recognized for his achievements in quan-
tum dynamics and nuclear
physics. While teaching in Rome,
Fermi discovered element 93,
neptunium, and conducted studies
of beta radioactivity based on the
transformation of protons into
neutrons. Awarded the Nobel Prize
in 1938, Fermi and his Jewish wife
fled from the Stockholm ceremony
to the United States. While a professor at the University of Chicago,
Fermi unleashed the first self-
sustaining chain reaction of ura-
nium. An initiator of the atomic era,
Fermi was a participant in one of
the most awesome events of this
century, the detonation of the first
hydrogen bomb on July 16, 1945.
Today, Fermi's work in nuclear
physics is being elaborated on by
another Italian Nobel winner, Carlo
Rubbia, director of the European
Space Nuclear Research Center.

The Olivetti Praxis
48. The 75-year-old
Italian company is
Europe's leading
manufacturer of
computers and
word processors.

A page of weaponry design from Leonardo da Vinci's Codex Atlanticus. The Renaissance genius was a skilled inventor and engineer.

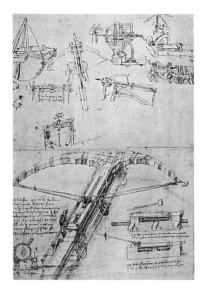

His work deals with the process of creating new subatomic particles within a special accelerator.

If the Italians have distinguished themselves in physics, formulating nature's laws and pondering its unseen forces, they are also masters of the applied sciences which render life easier, richer, more enjoyable and exciting. The name "Olivetti," for example, is synonymous with the rapid and accurate diffusion of language. The largest

Susterman's portrait of Galileo, whose experiments in telescopy corroborated the Copernican theory of planetary revolution around the sun.

manufacturer of electronic typewriters, computers and word-
processors in Europe, Olivetti is a
seventy-five-year-old company. Its
founder, Camillo Olivetti, was a
pioneer in Italian design who
insisted that a typewriter is not a
"knick-knack for a drawing room"
but should look "elegant and
serious." Today, many Olivetti designs are considered classics. The
"Lexicon" and flame-red "Valentine" typewriters, esteemed for their
style and efficiency, are represented in the collection of the New
York Museum of Modern Art.

It is especially in the design and
manufacture of automobiles that
the Italians are renowned for excellence. "Alfa Romeo," "Ferrari,"
"Lamborghini," "Bugatti," are
names that epitomize the absolute
ultimate in elegance and freedom
of speed.

The Italians are unrivalled in the
production of super-driving machines which are cunningly luxurious. The sleek, lithe design of these
cars has a distinctive glamour,
their very appearance suggesting
a mood of flight. The rhythmic
drive, the hum, surge, and thrust of
the Italian engine are legendary,
proven in races and coveted by
auto enthusiasts the world over. As
early as 1909, the Italian futurist,
Filippo Marinetti, praised the special dynamism and grace of the
Italian racing car, more beautiful,
he felt, than the Winged Victory of
Samothrace. The automobile,
symbol of velocity, is also the ultimate symbol of our twentieth century lifestyle. The tradition of the
Italian car is rooted in the progress
of this century—Bugatti originated
in 1909, Lancia in 1906, Fiat in 1907,
Alfa Romeo in 1910, Maserati in
1926, Ferrari in 1940, and Lamborghini in 1963. Each of these
magnificent machines represents
man's pride in energy, the ecstasy
of motion.

Moto Guzzi V7 Spe-
cial—an emblem of
youth, speed, and
freedom.

Margaret Courtney-Clarke

Italians are unsur-
passed in the manu-
facture of coveted
sports cars, which
combine sleek
beauty and ad-
vanced technology.

Margaret Courtney-Clarke

Soccer

Soccer is a source of Italian national pride and competitive spirit. Whether it is a Sunday match or a World Cup championship, *calcio* is the passion and the favorite pastime of the Italian people.

Every Sunday, from the second week of September until the end of May, the sport of soccer rules the nation of Italy. For that one day each week, nearly half the Italian population either goes to the stadium, listens on the radio, or watches their favorite game on television.

They call it *calcio* in Italy. And when the Italian people aren't watching, reading, arguing, or betting on it, there are a good many of them out there playing the game. It's the passion and pastime of the Italian people. Every week, billions of lire are bet in a legal football pool known as *Totocalcio*. Four national newspapers devote almost all of their pages to following the sport. Hundreds of magazine and television stories follow every move of the great players. People spend up to twenty dollars or fifteen pounds a seat in the capacity stadiums, in a nation where the professional teams stop at nothing to buy and assemble some of the greatest football talent in the world.

The Italian league is known as the wealthiest and most competitive of all professional leagues. Only two foreigners are allowed on the roster of each club. German, British, French, Argentinian, Irish, and Brazilian players all sell their talents for top dollar in Italy and Europe. Yet the greatest Italian soccer players almost always stay home. Pride for the game drives almost everyone involved.

First Division soccer in Italy, known as "Series A," is made up of the sixteen top professional teams in the country. They play amongst themselves from September until May to determine the national champion. It's a hotly contested league, with enormous rivalries between the opposing cities. And the competition stays tough from year to year by a seasonal rotation of the teams with the best record of performance.

The three weakest teams in Series A are dropped from Division 1 into the Second Division, Series B. And likewise, the top teams with the best records in Series B move up and become First Division competitors. This system goes right on down through all the minor divisions of professional soccer in Italy, and helps keep the competitive edge remarkably honest.

While the professional leagues try to maintain their own standard of excellence on the field, it's the fans that fuel a fierce and deeply personal sense of honor in the performance of their local heroes.

The great players in Italy are praised and ridiculed like gods.

Maradonna, the brilliant South American centerfielder, was bought by Naples for eight million dollars or over five million pounds from the Barcelona club. When he signed with Naples and was introduced at a press conference at the stadium, over 70,000 Naples fans packed the stands, just to get a look at him. There was no game, no exhibition. Just Maradonna.

In every city all over Italy, Sunday afternoon automobiles and buses are filled with singing, chanting calcio fans, wearing their team scarves and hats, hanging madly out the windows waving the club flag. The wins and losses of the hometown heroes have now come to represent all the stubborn feudal pride that divided the nation of Italy up until the late nineteenth century, when the country was finally unified. This same fierce regionalism still plays itself out, Sunday after Sunday, on the fields of the stadiums. The competition is so intense between rival teams, it often moves fans to violence in the stands. In the history of soccer itself, this comes as no surprise.

Modern soccer, or "football," as it is known, owes its present origins to the British. The official game as we know it was born at the Freemason's Tavern in London on October 26, 1863. The ceremony was more or less a friendly "rules agreement" between the many adherents of the sport being played, including soccer's close relative, rugby. The British gave it the name "Association Football," which in short form and with accent, became the slang of "assoc," and grew into the word "soccer."

Yet whatever name one gives the game, soccer might very well be one of man's oldest true sports. Primitive soccer was essentially a barbarian activity, a blood sport

involving countless participants, oftentimes the ancient victors in battle, who celebrated the event by kicking the severed heads of their opponents around the field of victory.

Eventually an inflated animal bladder took the place of head-kicking, and the ancient Chinese, Hopi Indians, Incas, Egyptians, Japanese, and Africans all played their own versions of the game. Usually, it involved great numbers of people vaguely separated into two sides, trying at all cost to get the poor bladder to a cliff, or a river, or some natural appointed boundary.

Julius Caesar had his Roman legions play a variation of the game known as *Harpastan*. It was a military exercise, primarily meant to condition his soldiers. A single ball would be tossed among roughly five hundred men, and they were left to fight it out amongst themselves until completely exhausted.

The Roman game went to Britain during the days of the Holy Empire, and then returned formally to Italy in 1892, when British residents started up the "Il Vecchio Genoa." It was a football club that refused Italians membership until 1897. At nearly the same time in Milan, British businessmen started an organization welcoming Italians, known as the Milan Cricket and Football Club.

By the turn of the century, calcio was played nearly everywhere in Italy. It's the simplest of games, needing only a ball and a handful of players. Italian people took to playing in the streets and the countryside, and eventually developed their own national style.

The premier event of professional soccer is of course the World Cup Tournament. Organized in 1930, the World Cup is played every four years, as an elimination tourna-

ment of over one hundred international teams. Italy has won the World Cup three times. Only Brazil, with the immortal Edson Arantes de Nascimento—Pele, the greatest goal scorer of all time—has won as many.

Italy won her first Cup in 1934, in Rome, and Mussolini turned the event into a parade of fascist glory. The players wore black uniforms and went undefeated to gain their first leg on the Cup. They won again in Paris, in 1938. And then after the war, with very high hopes in the 1950 tournament, the brilliant Torino team, with many of Italy's top players, was wiped out in a devastating air crash.

Pele and his Brazilian teammates dominated World Cup play

through the late fifties and sixties, winning three times, and becoming the first nation to retire the Cup. Finally, in 1982, the "Azzuri," Team Italia, coached by the great Enzo Bearzot, won their third World Cup. This team was a collection of Italy's greatest professionals.

World Cup victories or not, calcio in Italy is the predominant sport of the people. It represents as much modern legend and passion as the Italians can possibly give to their national pastime. Operating as a multi-billion lire industry, it lives deep in the hearts of all its fans. A simple, fluid, brilliant game, whether it's in the street, the schoolyard, or the capacity stadiums, calcio rules in the nation of Italy. To some, it is almost everything.

INVENTION AND SPORT

Margaret Courtney-Clarke

Cycling

Strong legs are a legacy in Italy, the result of mountainous topography and high-priced petrol. Bicycling is both a boon and a beneficiary of that legacy. Housewives pedaling to market with their shopping bags hanging from the handlebars is as common a sight as farmers rolling along with a melon tucked under one arm.

On weekends the roads are filled with cyclists. Alone, or in pairs, of either gender, and of all ages, these weekend riders sport the latest in cyclewear and the finest in bicycles. Many a visitor can recall a day when they were motoring along quietly and were suddenly surrounded by dozens, sometimes hundreds of earnest cyclists, their lean bodies bent over the handle-

bars, legs moving like well-oiled pistons, the riders seemingly a single organism as they swept by.

For the most part, these cyclists belong to local clubs that religiously schedule a two- to three-hour *giro* (trip) every week. They are as serious as they look as they deftly jockey for position in the pack, or sprint up an incline. These cyclists have techniques that they hope will one day help them win the exalted status of professional.

When it comes to rating Italian sports, soccer must share the spotlight with bicycling. While millions crowd the stadiums for soccer games, just as many line the routes of major cycle road races, cheering on their favorites. Helicopter-born TV crews bring the

competitions into Italian living rooms, where millions more watch them on the nightly newscast. Virtually every province has its own "tour," and the attention these races get is the sport's lifeblood, ample incentive for major promoters who recognize a substantial audience before whom they can display their trade names.

The Giro d'Italia is Italy's cycling World Series, a race encompassing over 3,300 kilometers that begins in Sicily and ends in Milan. It is made up of stages or segments, and the racers must complete one each day. Like other European races, it is long and hard, the ultimate test of stamina and determination. The Giro d'Italia is usually held in May, its twenty-two stages occupying

Bicycling is considered "big business" in Italy. The Italian racing teams are not only recognized for their incomparable skill, but for the superiority of their equipment.

Racing at top speed around the track, these cyclists compete with split-second precision as they sprint within inches of each other toward the finish line.

most of the month as riders pedal their way north.

The racers must cope with varied terrain. On easier days, they roll on flat highways. More often they struggle through steep mountain passes. Their muscular legs tighten as they climb to crests from which they will plummet through serpentine turns at speeds that exceed sixty miles an hour.

They ride in tandem with danger. Even their superbly conditioned physiques will not be able to absorb the punishment should they skid, fall, or collide at such speeds. Injury notwithstanding, the regimen is physically taxing. Racers easily shed as many as ten pounds in a single day, and only recoup the lost body weight by consuming gargantuan meals each night.

The best of these professionals earn millions, but it is a hard-earned wealth. They participate in one or two races every day, competing five days out of every seven during the season. Off-season, they stay in shape by clocking as many as 150 miles daily, and average 20,000 in a single year. Their physiques are lean, with as little as four percent body fat, and their pulse rates idle along at a comatose forty beats per minute.

In many ways, Italian cycling is like American boxing. A few of the very best earn fame and fortune. Unlike boxing, however, even the average Italian can enjoy this sporting passion, and many do. To cycle among racers and amateur cyclists is to participate in one of life's more important activities. Italian cyclists respond immediately to fellow travellers with warmth and respect, and a visiting cyclist should always allow extra time in his or her schedule to enjoy this special attention.

Shopkeepers want to know where one is going, how far one has come, and what kind of bike is

being used. Italian cyclists will pull alongside, and they chatter as easily as they pedal, their determination and friendship bridging any language barrier. They readily go out of their way to see strangers safely to their destination, and there are many visiting cyclists whose pleasant memories include an evening that resulted from an impromptu invitation to dinner.

In addition to being a country where biking predominates, Italy is also the premier country in bicycle design and production. Among cyclists the world over, Italy is known for preeminence in bike design and workmanship. Guercotti, Cinelli, Detto Pietro, Sergal—these are names of bicycles and equipment without peer. To own a bike whose components have all been made by Campagnolo is to own the best, a responsive thoroughbred whose price tag easily exceeds $2500.

Although Italians themselves are not fond of cycle touring, visitors rank Italy as the least expensive European country to see while pedaling. A savvy cyclist comes prepared to this land of mountains. Physical conditioning—earned on a bike beforehand—and a fifteen-speed bicycle are the only assurances that one will be overwhelmed by this country's beauty rather than by its topography.

May and September are the best times to tackle Italian touring, unless one can accommodate the ninety-degree temperatures that prevail during midsummer, especially south of Rome. North of the eternal city, a cyclist will encounter cooler temperatures but should be prepared to cope with traffic, especially on coastal and mountain roads in and around the industrial city centers. The bonus in either course is ever present sunshine with nary a drop of rain to dampen the experience.

Chapter 10

Travel

Literary Impressions

Once upon a time there was The Grand Tour. Well-born young men (and upon occasion, well-chaperoned young ladies), accompanied by a tutor and carrying the works of Cicero and Sophocles, set out to complete their education. Whether observing the inscrutable sphinx or standing in the shadow of the Parthenon, the traveler was obliged to be guided and additionally inspired by words of the sage.

Then, in 1826, the English writer Mary Shelley wrote, "there is a new generation of travelers...who understand the language...who more easily adjust to the food, the temperament. They have lesser dependence on guidebooks and dates, and a greater interest in the natives."

Over a century later E.M. Forster remarked: "The traveler who has gone to Italy to study the tactile values of Giotto or the corruption of the Papacy, may return remembering nothing but the blue sky and the men and women who live under it."

On Monday, July 1, 1844, Charles Dickens transported his entire menage to Genoa and ensconced them in the Palazzo Peschiere (Palace of Fishponds). Although it was a "domestic excursion" rather than a tour of monuments, Dickens traveled extensively during that year and his correspondence dealt with "the liveliest impressions of novelty and freshness" rather than political views or even reassessments of Italian artistic treasures.

"I had been half afraid to go to Verona, lest it should at all put me

This row of ancient columns in Pompeii provides a glimpse into an illustrious past civilization.

Some of the detailed and imaginative statuary that fills the buildings and cathedrals of Parma.

out of conceit with Romeo and Juliet...but the misgiving vanished ...it is so...picturesque a place... fantastic buildings...a romantic town! I walked through and through the town. There is a modern theater where they performed the opera of Romeo and Juliet...I read (it) in my own room at the inn that night."

But, he felt: "There is nothing in Italy, more beautiful to me, than the coast road between Genoa and Spezzia...on the one side there is the free blue sea, on the other are lofty hills, ravines, besprinkled with white cottages, patches of dark olive woods, country churches with their light open towers and country houses gaily painted...wild cactus and aloe in exuberant profusion...gardens...blushing...with clusters of the Belladonna."

He was particularly fond of one of the fishing villages, Camoglio, with "its little harbor on the sea, hundreds of feet below the road... descended into by the winding mule-tracks, a primitive seafaring town; the saltiest, roughest, most piratical little place."

He visited the marble quarries of Carrara on a pony. "Imagine the clumsy carts of five hundred years ago, being used to this hour, and drawn, as they used to be, five hundred years ago, by oxen, whose ancestors were worn to death five hundred years ago...." "Two pair...twenty pair, to one block, according to its size...."

Later that day, standing in a sculptor's studio, ne was struck that "...those exquisite shapes should grow out of all this toil and sweat and torture!"

Margaret Courtney-Clarke

Speaking of creating, Mark Twain noted in *Innocents Abroad* that "...the Creator made Italy from designs by Michelangelo."

The overwhelming sensuality experienced by D.H. Lawrence (who lived in Lago de Garda from the autumn of 1912 to the spring of 1913) was captured in "Twilight in Italy." "The day was gone, the twilight was gone, and the snow was invisible as I came down to the side of the lake. Only the moon, white and shining, was in the sky, like a woman glorying in her own loveliness as she loiters superbly to the gaze of all the world, looking sometimes through the fringe of dark olive leaves, sometimes looking at her own superb, quivering body, wholly naked in the water of the lake."

From Palermo, Lawrence took a "long, slender, old steamer" to the island of Sardinia and Cagliari. "We go down from the chill upper deck. It is growing full of day. Bits of pale gold are flying among delicate but cold flakes of cloud from the east, over Monte Pellegrino, bits of very new turquoise sky come out. Palermo on the left crouches upon her alt-harbor—a little desolate, disorderly, end-of-the-world, end-of-the-sea, along her quay front.

"The land passes slowly, very slowly. It is hilly, but barren looking, with a few trees. And it is not spikey and rather splendid, like Sicily. Sicily has style. We keep along the east side of the body—away in the west is Cape Spartivento. And still no sight of Cagliari." Then, " . . . suddenly there is Cagliari: a naked town rising steep, steep,

The clean, cool lines and stark whiteness of this Mediterranean villa on the island of Panarea, located off the coast of Sicily, are a welcome contrast to the hot sun overhead and the azure blue sea below.

golden-looking, piled naked to the sky from the plain at the head of the formless hollow bay. It is strange and rather wonderful . . . not a bit like Italy."

And, finally, in the town: "Strange, stony Cagliari. We climbed up a street like a corkscrew stairway. And we saw announcements of a children's fancy-dress ball. Imagine a street like a corkscrew stair paved with slippery stone. And imagine two bay horses rowing their way up it. The spirit of the place is a strange thing. Our mechanical age tries to override it. But it does not succeed."

At Cagliari's market: "Eggs in these great round dish-baskets of golden brass: but eggs in piles, in mounds, in heaps, a Sierra Nevada of eggs, glowing warm white. How they glow! . . . myriads of eggs, glowing avenues of eggs."

Local women: "They are amusing . . . so brisk and defiant . . . on the alert. You feel they would fetch you a bang over the head as leave as look at you. Tenderness, thank heaven, does not seem to be a Sardinian quality. Italy is so tender—like cooked macaroni—yards and yards of soft tenderness ravelled round everything. Here . . , (men) don't make those great leering eyes, the inevitable yours-to-command look of Italian males. . . . men (here) look at these women . . . it is Mind-yourself, my lady. These women have to look out for themselves . . . Man is going to be male Lord if he can . . . in these women there is something shy and defiant and un-get-atable."

On a morning commuter train heading to Messina, Lawrence made an observation on the young men: "Each one thinks he is as handsome as Adonis, and as 'fetching' as Don Juan. Extraordinary! . . . and, if a few trouser-buttons are missing, or if a black hat perches above a thick black

The Umbrian town of Orvietto perches precariously above a bluff.

Margaret Courtney-Clarke

A pensive *giovinetto* gazes mournfully into the camera, as does the weather-worn lion above him.

A wary tom stands guard over his master's gondola.

muffler and a long excruciated face, it is all the course of nature."

"This is the soul of the Italian since the Renaissance. In the sunshine he basks asleep, gathering up a vintage into his veins which in the nighttime he will distill into ecstatic sensual delight, the intense, white-cold ecstasy of darkness and moonlight, the raucous, cat-like destructive enjoyment, the senses conscious and crying out in their consciousness in the pangs of the enjoyment, which has consumed the southern nation, perhaps all the Latin races, since the Renaissance."

The Irish novelist Sean O'Faolain spent the summer of 1948 traveling around Italy and, in his book, *A Summer in Italy*, noted: "To the Italians, who live life to the full, brimming it over, throwing their whole bodies and souls into everything they do, life must be an indivisible oneness; whereas we, of this forbidding North, who measure and strain, tuck God away in the Church and Venus away in the bed, and miserably and foolishly drain each part of life of the richness of the other."

O'Faolain's impression of Genoa was very distinct from Dickens's: "Genoa is no tourist city, with polite cafe quarters, urbane piazzas, suave waiters in white aprons, leisurely Pernods, dainty ices, bands to entertain the ladies, quiet gossips over morning coffee, guides, carrozzas, gondoliers, vine-shaded restaurants, discreet gardens, long moonings over river-walls while the Arno or the Po or the Tiber whispers by. It is a devil-town; a seaman's whore. It is the best port in the Mediterranean for a sailor's money from Gib [Gibraltar] to Port Said. If you want to see life pullulating like an ant-heap, go to Genoa."

And, "Back behind the fashionable strip of coastline, the impor-

Colorful umbrellas and lounges await sunbathers on the beach at Calabria.

tant trees are not the myrtle, tamarisk, oleander, pine, yucca, peach, palm or ilex, decorative trees. What counts here are figs, olives, sweet chestnuts, almonds and vines. When flour is scarce, as it almost always is, the people up in the hills will subsist on dried figs and on flour made from the sweet chestnuts."

And the people: "The Italian gives heart to his work . . . (they) have a gift for enjoying life . . . their rages die in them, their passions flood out and are gone."

Travel by train afforded ample opportunity for observing the people. Lawrence believed, "It's much the nicest way, travelling third-class on the railway. There is space, there is air, and it is like being in a lively inn, everybody in good spirit." O'Faolain opined, "An Italian wagon-lit in summer is as hot and friendly as an Italian tenement . . . . All you have to do is to stand in the corridor and pick up life stories for the listening."

The Irishman in Venice: "I take a gondola and go out on the south-ern lagoon, to my golden goddess as I have done every night since I came. Then she was frail and slight as a virgin; tonight she is breasted like a mother, but still I do not know whether it is I who am trembling or she, like lovers when the long marriage-day is at last done . . . The distant bell-tower of San Giorgio Maggiore is a stalk of blackness that at once invokes the bright immensity above and surrenders to the dark immediately below . . . the only sound is the whispering and lapping of the water, the oar

A visitor is raucously greeted by the pigeons of Piazza San Marco.

turning . . . and the impatient breathing of the gondolier. Has this summer night no end? . . .
shall we float farther and still farther south . . . out between the forts south and into the open Gulf, to the horizon of the Adriatic . . .
until the moon grows pale at the doorway of the Orient where even now the waters are beginning to feel the chill of dawn?"

But what of an Italian's view of why foreigners flock to his land? Luigi Barzini in *The Italians* queried, "What then is the fatal spell of Italy?"

Barzini mentioned that to Lord Byron all the women in Venice were spectacularly beautiful—one in particular, with her large black eyes and the figure of a Juno, dark hair streaming in the moonlight. But his colleague Shelley assessed Byron's conquests thusly, "perhaps the most contemptible of all who exist under the moon, the most ignorant, the most disgusting . . . they smell so strongly of garlic . . . ."

Whose impression is accurate, and, moreover, does it matter? Enchantment engulfs and submission takes many forms, as Barzini related in a tale of a bomber pilot who, returning from a mission, was about to jettison unused bombs over the church of San Giovanni Rotondo, and hesitated when he saw a bearded figure, arms upraised, gesturing a halt. The pilot didn't drop the bombs. After the war he met the friar at the church and converted to Catholicism.

Heinrich Heine remarked: "Simply letting yourself live is beautiful in Italy. In these marble palazzi sighs have a more romantic echo than in our modest brick houses; in the shade of these laurel bushes it is more pleasant to weep than under our gloomy fir trees; it is sweeter to daydream following the shapes of Italian clouds than under

The pale morning light shimmers on Lago de Garda, a quiet testament to its literary worth. The lake has been the subject of the attentions of D. H. Lawrence and other travellers who have succumbed to its beauty.

The morning mist slowly rises over a rain forest valley in Urbino.

the ash gray dome of a German sky, a workday sky in which even clouds take on the solemn and sulky expression of little burghers and yawn with boredom."

The pleasure of Italy for Henry James was: "the incomparable wrought fusion, fusion of human history and moral passion with the elements of earth and air, of color, composition, and form; that constitute her appeal and give it supreme heroic grace."

For Stendhal Italy was: "that combination of love, sensuality and sincerity . . . music lives only in Italy. In this beautiful country one must only make love; other pleasures of the soul are cramped here. Love here is delicious. Anywhere else it is only a bad copy."

This typical Italian town perches above the river banks.

Friuli-Venezia Giulia

Most people who claim to be Italophiles are totally unaware of the existence of Friuli-Venezia Giulia. They mistakenly believe that the eastern border of Italy is Venice and then, immediately, there is Yugoslavia. Perhaps a few ponder, for a moment or two, the whereabouts of Trieste. But how many know that Friuli is a region like Lombardy or Tuscany?

I had been planning an autumn trip to Italy and was contemplating visiting Milan. A chance meeting, a few provocative statements, and I was changing my itinerary. All I could find in the travel folders and brochures was that Friuli-Venezia Giulia "has a terrain that affords ample opportunities for those who enjoy mountains as well as sea-shore," and that "there are ruins of the ancient Roman city of Aquileia." Italy, at the very least, I reasoned, is the land of culture and climate, where one can *mangiare bene* and shop for beautiful leather goods. So why not take a chance and discover the unique treasures of mysterious Friuli? After all, if worse came to worse, I could always pack my bag and head for that well-travelled city nearby, Venice.

Not only did I not need alternate plans, I fell in love. A *raffinatezza* (refinement) characterizes the area — from the food and wines, to the conduct of the people, to the works of art. Twenty or thirty paintings may crowd the wall in a gallery of the Louvre, yet only one may be truly exceptional. In Friuli there is no plethora, but what there is *is* exceptional. From the frescoes

This sleepy little fishing village is just one of hundreds that dot Italy's coastline.

Friuli-Venezia Giulia provides many opportunities for quiet reflection.

TRAVEL

A whitewashed abbey nestled among the autumnal colors of the vineyard below.

Quaglio painted in the seventeenth century to adorn the intimate Cappella del Monte (built as a side chapel to what was originally a sixteenth century palazzo but today serves as a bank), to a mosaic-encrusted fourth century crypt and a sixth century basilica in a small island fishing village. Each one is truly a gem.

And so I came to Friuli. It was a quiet Sunday in November. As the days unfolded I became increasingly aware of the profile of the people. Besides being conservative in dress they are extremely soft-spoken and gentle in manner, hospitable to strangers and reliable as professionals. They don't believe in grand entrances or drama. Even the most reknowned are modest.

In my pre-trip research I failed to uncover any great families like the Medicis or the Sforzas, whose do-

mains had been meccas for poets, painters, and philosophers. Why? When I got to Friuli and met the people, travelled throughout the region and learned some of the history, I began to understand. Arts flourish in a climate of stability. Friuli had been used as a political and economic football for millennia.

Even in the beginning the land of Friuli-Venezia Giulia was a corridor connecting the East and the West. Bronze and Iron Age settlements arose in the northern-most mountainous areas. The Celts (to whom the Friulani trace their origins), came in about the fourth century B.C. and decided to stay a while—about two centuries. There were incursions by bands of Ostrogoths and Visigoths. The Romans founded a great civilization and thrived here until the middle of the fifth century, when Attila and his

Huns put an incendiary end to the Pax Romana. The Lombards came and settled, and in between there were marauding Magyars. Then Charlemagne's Franks created outposts for the Holy Roman Empire—and that was just the beginning. The Venetians of the Most Serene Republic (Serenissima) arrived in 1420 and used Friuli as a buffer zone against the Turks and others for three-and-a-half centuries.

Besides the primitive settlements, the splendor of the Roman achievement, and the establishment of the Christianity, there were the centuries of continual skirmishes and battles, hoards of crusaders traversing the land, the rape of dense forests in the plains to provide wood for the Serenissima's fleet. There were earthquakes, fires, floods, and plagues. Nine times the Friulani suffered devastation. The last catastrophe was the earthquake of 1976, and, once again, they are rebuilding.

The region of Friuli-Venezia Giulia, in the northeast corner of Italy, lies between the Adriatic Sea on the south and two mountain ranges in the north, the Carnic Alps in the northwest and the Julian Alps in the northeast. On the west it is bounded by the Livenza and Tagliamento rivers and on the east by Yugoslavia. Almost fifty percent of the territory is either mountain or hill; the rest is flat plains. While not exactly the geographical center of Friuli, Udine, slightly southeast of center, is considered its heart. It is a manageable city of 100,000 in a region of about 1,250,000, and is elegant without being sumptuous. The site chosen for the first known building in Udine (*circa* 1500 B.C.) was on the lone hill in the plains. On this foundation succeeding fortifications were erected. In the tenth century a castle and fortress were already established. By the twelfth century a village began to form at the bottom of the hill, and by the thirteenth century there was a thriving town and Udine was designated the capital of Friuli. In the sixteenth century the present Castello was built on the hilltop. The Venetian Governors General resided on the hilltop from 1420 until Napoleon's troops crushed the Serenissima. Finally, the Austrians took possession in 1813 but were ousted in 1861 with Italian Unification.

Immediately at the foot of the ancient hill is the Piazza della Liberta, surrounded by the pink-and-white fifteenth century Loggia del Lionella, the sixteenth century Loggia Di San Giovanni, the monument to the Treaty of Campoformido. (Napoleon represented nationalism, but even with this treaty independence was almost a century away.) Wending my way down the network of cobbled streets that diverge from the Piazza, I came upon some scaffolding on the Via Lovaria. In the process of repairing the sixteenth century facade of a building, fourteenth century frescoes were being revealed. I turned left in front of the site and found myself on the Via Vittorio Veneto, which leads past the Duomo and into the Mercatovecchio—a way lined with stone arcades filled with dozens of elegant boutiques. *Raffinatezza* is applied to the way meat is displayed in the window of the butchershop, fresh fish are exhibited in the huge old fishhouse, and shopkeepers treat browsers as well as steady customers.

For a cup of coffee and a bit of gossip, the "in" spot is the Contarena Cafe on the corner of the Via Cavour. Fast food has made no real inroad in Fruili, and even a pizza is made to order. At the Bar and Pizzeria Odeon, senators and military cadets alike order the

The sun-splashed Piazza della Libertá in Udine, the heart of the Friuli-Venezia Giulia region.

Sunbathers gather to soak in the warmth and await a turn at *bocci*.

house specialty, a cheese-filled pie topped with fresh arugula.

Fine dining is commonplace and I had some wonderfully memorable meals. One drizzly midday I had a sumptuous *pranzo* in front of the fire at La Vedova. I learned from Signora when I ordered prosciutto San Danielle (reputed to be the best in Italy, and "Made in Friuli"), that if it is not hand sliced the subtle delicacy of the flavor is marred. This was followed by a *mezzo* portion of risotto and porcini. It was game season: quail, pheasant...venison won out. When the omnipresent, multitiered pastry cart was rolled out with apple strudel and almond and chocolate cakes, I prudently selected a dish of creamy lemon ice cream.

Giovanni Battista Tiepolo came to Udine in 1726 and painted the *Fall of the Rebel Angels* on the ceiling over the main stairs of the Palazzo Arcivesconile and decorated the Chapel of the Sacrament in the

cathedral. Archbishop Delfino was so impressed that the young artist received his first major commission, a cycle in the gallery of the Archbishop's Palazzo. In the Red Room of the tribunal chamber, the ceiling fresco is an extraordinary scene of *The Judgment of Solomon*, in which the infant is held aloft by an executioner brandishing a gleaming sword, and is surrounded by his real mother, dressed in bright, true colors, and the imposter whose garments are in a haze, suggesting an unsubstantial figure. The most striking element in these frescoes was Tiepolo's rejection of the prevailing dark, rich, baroque tonalities in favor of luminous pastels.

If you place a compass point on Udine and draw a circle, you notice that almost every part of the region is easily accessible within an hour's drive. It is only one hundred miles from the tip of the island of Grado in the Adriatic to the

Austrian border.

About a half hour's drive to the south is the sixteenth century walled city of Palmanova, a particular favorite of mine. To prevent incursions of Ottomans from the east and Germans from the north, the Venetians built a line of fortifications in the plains. In creating Palmanova, they were guided by the Renaissance concept of man as the center of his universe. Standing in the town piazza in the midst of eleven statues of Venetian Governors General, I, too, had that feeling. Nine avenues, with buildings three or four stories high, are neatly laid out from the center, creating nine points of a star, the shape of the exterior wall.

Aquileia was founded by the Romans in 181 B.C. as a base of operations for further expansion to the north and east, and as a bulwark against barbaric incursions. It became much more. Due to its location, on a river just north of the

Adriatic, it became the most important trading center of the Roman Empire. Factories and workshops were established to manufacture bricks and glassware, and to carve the treasured, imported amber.

By the fourth century Christianity was legalized and two splendid stone basilicas were constructed by the patriarch. The Huns completely destroyed both, leaving only the mosaic pavement. The foundation of one was the site of a new basilica which the Christians began to build in the fifth century. It is an artful composite of Romanesque and Gothic. I was particularly fascinated by the way the fourth century mosaic floor (with additions of the faces of later patrons) undulated like a wrinkled carpet because of the way the land has resettled after the numerous earthquakes. The attendant led me through a narrow stone passage, down a ramp and over a strip of wooden walkway. We were in the crypt of the other original basilica, which was not rebuilt. The floor is a menagerie of the animal kingdom: rams and peacocks, pheasants, lobsters, each perched on a tree. In the earliest Church iconography, the tree symbolized Christ's cross. The cross itself was not used because it represented shame, since common criminals were hanged there. It was not until after the year 1,000 that the cross was regarded as the symbol of sacrifice and incorporated into religious artwork.

When Attila sacked Aquileia, 100,000 survivors fled south to Grado. Driving to Grado from the mainland across the three-mile bridge that spans the lagoon, I watched gulls swooping through the breeze and around the thatched roofs of the *casoni* of the fishermen who live on tiny islets in the lagoon.

Strolling along narrow *calle* (ancient Venetian ways) brought me upon *campielli* (small squares) where I found a fountain, a cafe, and a shop or two. A cluster of Paleo-Christian buildings impose on a little piazza encircled by modest houses. The great Basilica of St. Euphemia dates to the sixth century. It, too, is paved in mosaics, but set amidst the geometric design are Latin inscriptions. The neighboring, smaller Basilica of St. Maria delle Grazie was built between the fourth and the sixth centuries, a prosperous period in Grado.

Just across the lagoon to the west is another seaside resort, presenting a totally different personality. Lignano is a collection of three districts, linked by the city bus. The most remote, and least populous, is Lignano Riviera. There are miles of isolated beaches, pine groves along sandy paths leading to white dunes and the sound of the gulls; perhaps in the distance a lone rider on a prancing stallion. Lignano Pineta boasts Hemingway Park, the creation of the noble Kechler family in honor of an old friend. Hemingway described Friuli during World War I in *A Farewell to Arms,* and later wrote about it in "Across the River and into the

Imposing yet subtle, this classically designed estate house in Udine is a perfect example of *raffinatezza.*

The facade of the Palazzo del Commune exemplifies the Venetian influence on this area.

Trees." He incorporated members of the Kechler family as well as details of their homes in his books. On a visit to Lignano, savoring the expanse of beaches and sensing the beginning of a hotel boom, he called it the "Florida" of Italy. The third community, Lignano Sabbiadoro (golden sand) has that and much more. During most of the year the city has five thousand residents; in summer it swells to over three hundred thousand. They

have a total of five million visitors.

In Lignano Sabbiadoro, there is the huge Luna Park, night clubs, discos, a health spa where you can be "buried in heated, pure white sand" or have a stimulating underwater massage, and hundreds of restaurants and bars. Canals dissecting the peninsula create marinas for thousands of boats, and an ambiance for scores of sidewalk cafes. Even during a brisk November sunset, a couple of

local folk carrying glasses of warming grappa sat at a harbor-side table and watched some clouds drift east toward Trieste.

In Roman times, when Udine was a mere fortress, the coast around Trieste was dotted with splendid villas. I approached the city with great anticipation. In 1719 it was made a free port by the Hapsburgs and flourished in the eighteenth and nineteenth centuries. Up until the time that it was annexed to Italy at the end of World War I, it had been an enormously vital and thriving community. I was already aware that the hub of the city is the hill of San Giusto, with its cathedral built on fifth century foundations and its grand gothic rose window, and of course there is a treasury and a fourteenth century bell tower. There is a castle filled with armor, artworks, Flemish tapestries, and legendary dungeons. A Roman theater dates from the first century A.D. and the Verdi Theatre was built in 1801. What I wanted to do was walk through the streets and discover the texture of the city. I started in the Piazza dell'Unita d'Italia at the Cafe degli Specchie—a favorite haunt of a one-time resident, James Joyce. Undeterred by the chilling breezes at the exposed sidewalk cafe, determined sippers and sundae snackers read their *Corriere della Seras.* I wandered through its district, exploring secondhand book-stores and antiques shops (which are virtually non-existent in Friuli). Earlier in the afternoon I had visited the castle and grounds of Miramare, which had been built for the Archduke Maximillian of Hapsburg and his wife, Carlotta of Belgium. To create the verdant parkland, soil had been brought in to cover the rocks on the promontory of the isolated site on the *Costiera,* just north of the city. The garden is filled with imports: sequoias from California, cedars from Lebanon, and African tamarinds. Masses of wisteria, maidenhead, and fern frame the walks rambling past ponds and the charming casetta on the hilltop where the couple lived until their residence was ready for occupancy in 1860.

Venzone was my next stop. Here I visited the restored fifteenth century town hall with its splendid loggia, spanned by heavy oak beams and adorned with local coats of arms. I passed cranes on worksites temporarily enclosed with protective fences. One site in particular lured me. I had heard about some vintage mummies on display, and on my drive to the Alps stopped for a look. It seems that when moving sarcophagi in the small chapel of the Duomo in the last century, thirteen mummified bodies were discovered. The deaths occurred between 1704 and 1878. A dwarf who died during the Black Plague in 1348 had been discovered during an earlier excavation in 1647. (A seepage of water and air into the coffins caused a special fungus to grow: *Hipha Ombicini Pers.* Within approximately one year the body dries and the skin becomes parchment.)

Driving north, I moved on to Tolmezzo and the Ethnographic Museum of Carnia which is situated in a huge seventeenth century palazzo on the main street.

Terrain and climate dictated development of craft skills that sustained the people in this area. Since the middle of the fifteenth century there had been an outstanding tradition of master woodcarvers. (They would carve during the hard winters, and in the spring, cross the Alps and sell their work in Austria and Germany.) Magnificent baroque altars with intricately detailed panels are in churches throughout the hills. Because there were no local sources for precious stones, the wood itself was treated as a treasure. In the museum I saw walnut chests carved and inlaid; wardrobes, benches, and huge matrimonial beds. The carnation, symbol of marriage, and the sun are recurring motifs. I was told that the Celtic traditions are alive and thriving. To mark the winter solstice men still gather on nearby hilltops and throw down cidulis, flaming palm-sized wood discs, "to kill the darkness."

To assuage my hunger I stopped at the highly recommended local Albergo Roma for some Carnic specialties, prepared with loving *raffinatezza* by the chef. Among the assortment I recall *frico,* a very thin, very crispy wedge of grated Montasio cheese and potatoes, pan-fried in a light oil. There was a fascinating dish of warm, fermented turnips topped with strips of pork sausage. Tiny roasted quail were accompanied by the regional mainstay, polenta. And ahhh, the wines....

By the year 1,000, the barbarians had destroyed the vineyards which the Romans had planted. At the end of the eleventh century, a group of Benedictine monks began restoring and nurturing the vines. Today, Dr. Walter Filiputti lives

The midday sun illuminates this typical Friulian piazza.

The approach to this humble villa promises conviviality and fabulous food within.

in their thousand-year-old stone abbey, Abbazia di Rosazzo and is the managing director of the extensive vineyards, which have belonged to the Archbishop of Udine since the eighteenth century. Friuli's production is small but excellent. Recently they have been winning an increasing number of gold medals in the highly competitive wine world. With sparkling Spumante, Verduzzo, Tokai, Ribolla, Merlot (and its subtle scent of raspberry), the fragrant dessert wine Frangolino, and grappa—which they have refined to a sophisticated eau de vie—they are a vital force on the world market.

As I travelled further north, a decidedly Alpine flavor appeared: iron balconies were replaced by carved wooden ones, church steeples had an Eastern contour, the townsfolk were bundled up in loden coats and lederhosen. My destination was Tarvisio, where majestic mountain chains converge and, since the last century, an internationally

prominent ski area is located. Because it is on the northeastern border of Italy there is easy access to ski slopes in both Austria and Yugoslavia.

There are dozens of slopes and ski trails in the mountain ranges. Cable cars lift you above alpine villages and through gorges to the frosty peaks where fields of edelweiss grow. Cross-country skiing is possible through May and there is year-round skiing at Sella Nevea. In the summer you can take off your skis at a mountain top *refugio* which is outfitted with beds and a stove, prepare some food and enjoy the vast panorama of mountainsides and valleys, blanketed with a rainbow of protected flowers, the red and white lilies, primroses, gentian, cowslip, and golden narcissus.

In 50 B.C., Julius Caesar founded Cividale, where the Patriarch fled after the sacking of Aquileia. It is the Lombard influence that has left a particular heritage here. I walked up the narrow path high above the trout-filled Natisone River and entered the door of the eighth century sanctuary built by a Lombard queen. A couple of fifth century Roman columns were installed in the tiny chapel. The walls are covered in frescoes from the eighth, twelfth, and fourteenth centuries. A wooden stall was introduced when the Sisters in the adjacent convent used the chapel for their prayers. But the cross-vaulted ceiling is the most remarkable element. It is covered with gold mosaics and precious stones that have shed their sparkle in the centuries.

A barkeep loaned me a large iron key. I walked next door and used it to enter a fourth century Celtic funeral crypt dating from the fourth century. Bending low, I descended the stairs and wandered through the chambers. Three large

masks are carved into the stone walls. The faces have gaping mouths, a symbol representing the last human breath. There are shelves cut into the stone where the urns containing human ashes were placed. The Romans had used this consecrated ground as a jail and then the Lombards converted it into a storehouse.

After my morning's activities I stopped in at Zorutti's. Known for their grilled steaks and the Mazze di Tamburo (mushrooms that often weigh two pounds or more), I knew exactly what to order.

A pilgrims' route lies between Cividale and Castelmonte. Driving up the winding mountain road, mist encroaching on miles of vineyards, I passed a dozen or so Byzantine-style roadside altars tucked in the shadow of dense cherry groves.

Gorizia lies in the low, rolling, green hills of Collio on the eastern border. Actually it is a city divided—part of it is in Yugoslavia. Traces of the Middle Ages are everywhere: preserved stone houses, massive city walls, and the Castello Lantieri-Levetzow, where a stone tower has been incorporated into the rest of the mansion.

There's so much more of Friuli to be discovered. I want to return to Lignano in spring and ride horseback over the dunes and through the pines, or in summer and frolic in the world's biggest splash park, or sail through the islands of the lagoon and drift on the Natissa River up to Aquileia. An international air show is held at Aviano at the end of June. Individuals and squadrons perform stunts, and the famous Italian acrobatic squadron, Frecce Tricolri, are "breath-stoppers."

On the first Sunday in October I would be at the sprawling Villa Manin (home of the last Venetian Doge) for the mammoth Antiquities

Fair. Of course, I'd return to Trieste to experience the Sound and Light presentation at Miramare, and then I'd venture down to the depths of the Grotto Gigante. I want to explore the Cave of San Giovanni d'Antro, which is cut into a rocky mountainside and in which a chapel was created in the fifteenth century. In summer there are weekly berry festivals in the villages of Carnia and, in the autumn, there are porcini hunts. Even the presidents of Austria, Yugoslavia, and Italy join the throngs who participate in the huge Open Frontier day the second Sunday in September. Tre Confirmi, in the Carnic Alps, is the locale for folk singing and dancing and dining on spaghetti, goulash, and cevapcici. And, wouldn't it just be wonderful to go to the School of Mosaics at Spilimbergo and commission a huge Roman bath?

The Celtic influence is apparent in this rustic thatched cottage.

Sources/Useful Addresses

UNITED STATES

BICYCLES

Bicycle USA
Tourfinder
Suite 209R
6707 Whitestone Road
Baltimore, MD 21207
(301) 944-3399
cycling tours of Italy

Cycles Peugeot
555 Gotham Parkway
Carlstadt, NJ 07072
(201) 460-7000

Mariano A. Lucca & Associates
144 West Ferry Street
Buffalo, NY 14213
(716) 882-0188

Stuyvesant Bicycle
326 Second Avenue
New York, NY 10010
(212) 254-9200

BOOKSTORES

Foreign News Department
142 West 42nd Street
New York, NY 10036
(212) 840-1868

Omnium Publishing Corporation
630 Third Avenue
New York, NY 10017
(212) 986-9023

Rizzoli Editore Corporation
712 Fifth Avenue
New York, NY 10019
(212) 397-3700

Vanni, S.F.
30 West 12th Street
New York, NY 10011
(212) 675-6336
books

CARS

Alfa Romeo Corporation
240 Sylvan Street
Englewood Cliffs, NJ 07632
(212) 736-6516
(800) 447-4700

Ferrari North America
777 Terrace Avenue
Hasbrouck Heights, NJ 07604
(201) 393-4081

Lamborghini
Meadowlands Car Imports
608 Tonnelle Avenue
North Bergen, NJ 07047
(212) 517-8111

CERAMICS & GLASS

Colony
225 Fifth Avenue
New York, NY 10010
(212) 924-7700

Conran's Inc.
160 East 54th Street
New York, NY 10022
(212) 371-2225

M. Das Company
The Gift Center
888 Brannan Street
Suite 332
San Francisco, CA 94103
(415) 626-6166

Dolfinger's Inc.
325 West Walnut
Louisville, KY 40202
(502) 893-3634

Firenze Imports, Inc.
3030 West Federal Street
Youngstown, OH 44510
(216) 743-3654

Gear
110 Seventh Avenue
New York, NY 10011
(212) 929-2622
stoneware

International Boutique Ltd.,
500 La Guardia Place
New York, NY 10012
(212) 677-0705

Lo Forti Imports
820 Mission Street
San Francisco, CA 94103
(415) 397-8220

Richard-Ginori
711 Fifth Avenue
New York, NY 10022
manufacturer, write for information

Riedel Crystal of America
24 Aero Road
Bohemia, NY 11716
(516) 567-7575

Villeroy & Boch Tableware
41 Madison Avenue
New York, NY 10010
(212) 639-1747

FASHION

Women's

Giorgio Armani
815 Madison Avenue
New York, NY 10021
(212) 988-9191

Bambola
9536 Wilshire Boulevard
Beverly Hills, CA 90212
(213) 273-7900
clothing, gifts, furniture

Barneys NYC
Seventh Avenue & 17th Street
New York, NY 10011
(212) 929-9000

Henri Bendel
10 West 57th Street
New York, NY 10019
(212) 247-1100
many collections

Benetton
601 Fifth Avenue
New York, NY 10017
(212) 752-2203
for store locations write:
767 Fifth Avenue
New York, NY 10153

Bergdorf Goodman
754 Fifth Avenue
New York, NY 10019
(212) 753-7300
many collections

Bloomingdales
1000 Third Avenue
New York, NY 10022
(212) 355-5900
Missoni boutique:
(212) 705-7486

Bottega Glasseia Ltd.
106 East Oak Street
Chicago, IL 60611
(312) 944-0981

Byblos
650 Fifth Avenue
New York, NY 10019
(212) 245-6750

Chez Catherine
210 Worth Avenue
Palm Beach, FL 33480
(305) 833-1600

Cicciobello
462 West Broadway
New York, NY 10012
(212) 475-1345

Colitti
225 Millburn Avenue
Millburn, NJ 07041
(201) 376-2129

Domani Inc.
12326 Olive Boulevard
St. Louis, MO 63141
(314) 434-3230

Fendi Roma
The Mall at Short Hills
Short Hills, NJ 07078
(201) 467-2727

Salvatore Ferragamo
717 Fifth Avenue
New York, NY 10022
(212) 759-3822

Gianfranco Ferré
414 North Rodeo Drive
Beverly Hills, CA 90210
(213) 271-5150

Fiorucci, Inc.
127 East 59th Street
New York, NY 10022
(212) 751-1404

Genny U.S.A. Inc.
650 Fifth Avenue
New York, NY 10019
(212) 245-4860
for location of nearest boutique:
(212) 308-2400

Gucci
685 Fifth Avenue
New York, NY 10022
(212) 826-2600
dresses, furs, gowns

Biltmore Fashion Park
2504 East Camelback Road
Phoenix, AZ 85016
(602) 957-8710

347 North Rodeo Drive
Beverly Hills, CA 90210
(213) 278-3451

South Coast Plaza
Costa Mesa, CA 92626
(714) 557-9600

Desert Fashion Plaza
Palm Springs, CA 92262
(619) 322-0880

253 Post Street
San Francisco, CA 94108
(415) 772-2522

9700 Collins Avenue
Bal Harbour, FL 33154
(305) 868-6504

256 Worth Avenue
Palm Beach, FL 33480
(305) 655-6955

Phipps Plaza
3500 Peachtree Road NE
Atlanta, GA 30326
(404) 233-4899

Hyatt Regency
2424 Kalakaua Avenue
Honolulu, HI 96815
(808) 923-2968

713 North Michigan Avenue
Chicago, IL 60611
(312) 664-5504

Somerset Mall
2881 Big Beaver Road
Troy, MI 48084
(313) 643-7630

Caesar's Palace
3570 Las Vegas Boulevard South
Las Vegas, NV 89101
(702) 731-1724

Caesar's Resort/Casino
55 Highway Fifty
Stateline, NV 89449
(702) 588-6278

Caesar's Hotel/Casino
2100 Pacific Avenue
Atlantic City, NJ 08404
(609) 347-6662

The Mall at Short Hills
Short Hills, NJ 07078
(201) 564-7600

Hattie Inc.
555 South Woodward
Birmingham, MS 48011
(313) 645-5755

I. Magnin
830 North Michigan Avenue
Chicago, IL 60611
(312) 751-0500

I. Santi
785 Madison Avenue
New York, NY 10021
(212) 535-9640

Krizia
805 Madison Avenue
New York, NY 10021
(212) 628-8180

150 Worth Avenue
Palm Beach, FL 33480
(305) 659-7154

Lady Battaglia
456 North Rodeo Drive
Beverly Hills, CA 90210
(213) 271-4728

The Magnin Company
323 North Rodeo Drive
Beverly Hills, CA 90210
(213) 273-5910

Missoni
836 Madison Avenue
New York, NY 10021
(212) 517-9339

Montenapoleone
789 Madison Avenue
New York, NY 10021
(212) 535-2660
lingerie and swimwear

Claire Pearone, Inc.
2771 Somerset Mall
Troy, MI 48084
(313) 643-0770

Saks Fifth Avenue
611 Fifth Avenue
New York, NY 10022
(212) 753-4000

Talese Town Shop
744 Asbury Avenue
Ocean City, NJ 08226
(609) 399–1035

Torie Steele Boutique
414 North Rodeo Drive
Beverly Hills, CA 90210
(213) 271–5150
children's and adults' clothing

The Twenty Four Collection
2399 Northeast Second Avenue
Miami, FL 33137
(305) 576–6424

Valentino
823–825 Madison Avenue
New York, NY 10021
(212) 772–6969

204 A Worth Avenue
Palm Beach, FL 33480
(305) 659–7533

600 New Hampshire Avenue
Washington, DC 20037
(202) 333–8700

Gianni Versace
816 Madison Avenue
New York, NY 10021
(212) 744–5572

437 North Rodeo Drive
Los Angeles, CA 90035
(213) 276–6799

97 Collins Avenue
Miami, FL 33154
(305) 864–0044

The Galleria at Crocker Center
70 Post Street
San Francisco, CA 94104
(415) 956–7977

Men's

Giorgio Armani
815 Madison Avenue
New York, NY 10021
(212) 988–9191

Barneys NYC
Seventh Avenue & 17th Street
New York, NY 10011
(212) 929–9000

Beau Brummel
410 Columbus Avenue
New York, NY 10024
(212) 874–6262

Bellocchio Uomo Ltd.
827 Madison Avenue
New York, NY 10021
(212) 472–1112

Cicciobello
462 West Broadway
New York, NY 10012
(212) 475–1345

David's
2213 Ala Moana Center
Honolulu, HI 96814
(808) 941–1031

Elysee
9521 Brighton Way
Beverly Hills, CA 90210
(213) 273–4127

Ermenegildo Zegna
9 West 57th Street
New York, NY 10019
(212) 751–3468
call or write for store locations

Salvatore Ferragamo
730 Fifth Avenue
New York, NY 10019
(212) 246–6211

Fiorente Uomo
960 Third Avenue
New York, NY 10022
(212) 759–5980

Walter Fong & Sons
459 Geary Street
San Francisco, CA 94102
(415) 397–7777

Lubiam U.S.A. Inc.
41 West 56th Street
New York, NY 10019
(212) 541–6331

Madonna-Sartorial, Inc.
223 East 60th Street
New York, NY 10022
(212) 832–0268

Polacheck's
227 East Wisconsin Avenue
Milwaukee, WI 03202
(414) 271–1007

Gino Pompeii Inc.
390 Fifth Avenue
New York, NY 10018
(212) 564–8900

Raleighs
1133 Connecticut Avenue NW
Washington, DC 20036
(202) 785–7071

Torie Steele Boutique
414 North Rodeo Drive
Beverly Hills, CA 90210
(213) 271–5150
children's and adults' clothing

Uomo Elegante
250 Fillmore
Denver, CO 80206
(303) 333–1414

Verri Uomo
802 Madison Avenue
New York, NY 10021
(212) 737-9200

Gianni Versace
816 Madison Avenue
New York, NY 10021
(212) 744–5572

437 North Rodeo Drive
Los Angeles, CA 90035
(213) 276–6799

97 Collins Avenue
Miami, FL 33154
(305) 864–0044

The Galleria at Crocker Center
70 Post Street
San Francisco, CA 94104
(415) 956–7977

FOOD & COOKING SUPPLIES

Balduccis
424 Avenue of the Americas
New York, NY 10011
(213) 673–2600
(800) 228–2028, ext. 72

Convito Italiano
11 East Chestnut
Chicago, IL 60611
(312) 943–2983
food and wine shop

Dean & De Luca Imports
121 Prince Street
New York, NY 10012
(212) 431–1691
mail order :

110 Greene Street
Suite 304
New York, NY 10012

Ferrara Foods & Confections, Inc.
195–201 Grand Street
New York, NY 10013
(212) 226–6150

Italian Food Center
186 Grand Street
New York, NY 10013
(212) 925–2954

Arthur G. Lombardi & Son, Inc.
P.O. Box 8724
New Haven, CT 06536
(203) 776–4853
wines

Manganaro Foods
488 Ninth Avenue
New York, NY 10018
(212) 563–5331

Patrician Foods
59–02 55th Street
Maspeth, NY 11378
(718) 381–8000

Perugina
636 Lexington Avenue
New York, NY 10017
(212) 688–2490
(800) 223–0039

Todaro Brothers
557 Second Avenue
New York, NY 10016
(212) 532–0633 *grocers*
(212) 679–7766 *mail order*

Williams-Sonoma
P.O. Box 7456
San Francisco, CA 94120
(415) 652–9007
*Imported cooking supplies and
   Italian specialty foods*

FURNISHINGS

Arquitectonica Products
142 Giralda Avenue
Coral Gables, FL 33134
(305) 446–3900
Memphis designs, among others

Atelier International, Ltd.
595 Madison Avenue
New York, NY 10022
(212) 644–0400
also carry lamps and fabrics

Axiom Designers
110 Greene Street
New York, NY 10021
(212) 219–2212
Brunati furniture

200 Kansas Street
Space 25
San Francisco, CA 94103
(415) 864–6688

Bel Vivere, Ltd.
8806 Beverly Boulevard
Los Angeles, CA 90048
(213) 278–1343

Beylerian, Ltd.
305 East 63rd Street
New York, NY 10021
(212) 755–6300

Campaniello Imports Ltd.
225 East 57th Street
New York, NY 10022
(212) 371–3700
Saporiti Italia

City
213 West Institute Place
Chicago, IL 60610
(312) 664–9581
Memphis designs, among others

Danco Design Associates
West Street
Routes 5 & 10
West Hatfield, MA 01088
(413) 247–5682

Danica House
100 West Micheltoreana Street
Santa Barbara, CA 93101
(805) 963–1441
leather sofas

Antonio Dell'Aglio
25 Southeast Second Avenue
Miami, FL 33131
(305) 358–2781
Giovanetti furniture importer

Di Carlo Furniture
263 Hanover Street
Boston, MA 02113
(617) 523–7991

Domus Inc.
5437-115 Fallwood Drive
Indianapolis, IN 46220
(317) 259–1350
distributors of Domus accessories

Engineered Custom Plastics
   Corporation
Division Kartell U.S.A.
P.O. Box 1000
Easley, SC 29640
(803) 859–1236

Estel Inc.
6695 Peachtree Street
Industrial Boulevard
Suite 212
Atlanta, GA 30360
(404) 446–0933

Giovanetti Furniture
The Merchandise Mart
Suite 841
Chicago, IL 60654
(312) 822–0346
Giovanetti distributor

Grace Designs
World Trade Center
#622
2050 Stemmons Freeway
Dallas, TX 75207
(214) 742–4320

Italdesign Center Inc.
Pacific Design Center
8687 Melrose Avenue
Suite 547
Los Angeles, CA 90069
(213) 659–6764
*Gruppo Industriale Busnelli leather
   seating importer*

Knoll International
655 Madison Avenue
The Knoll Building
New York, NY 10021
(212) 207–2200

Made in Italy Imports Inc.
1919 South Los Angeles Street
Los Angeles, CA 90015
(213) 746–2300

Walker & Zanger, Inc.
P.O. Box 241
Scarsdale, NY 10583
(914) 472–5666
Abet Laminate importer

Wallance Leisure Products
31 East Jefferson Street
Philadelphia, PA 19121
(215) 232–9900
Artexa carpeting importer

GENERAL ORGANIZATIONS

America-Italy Society
667 Madison Avenue
New York, NY 10022
(212) 838–1560

American Institute of Verdi Studies
Dept. of Music
New York University
24 Waverly Place
New York, NY 10003
(212) 598–3431

Italian Cultural Institute
686 Park Avenue
New York, NY 10021
(212) 879–4242

Italian Heritage and Culture
   Committee
686 Park Avenue
New York, NY 10021
(212) 988–4850

Italian Historical Society of America
111 Columbia Heights
Brooklyn, NY 11201
(718) 852–2929

United States Consulate Generals
101 Tremont Street
Boston, MA 02108
(617) 542–0483

500 North Michigan Avenue
Chicago, IL 60611
(312) 467–1550

11761 San Vicente Boulevard
Suite 911
Los Angeles, CA 90024
(213) 826–5998

231 Carondelet Street
New Orleans, LA 70130
(504) 524–2771

690 Park Avenue
New York, NY 10021
(212) 737-9100

421 Chestnut Street
Philadelphia, PA 19106
(312) 592-7329

2590 Webster Street
San Francisco, CA 94115
(415) 931-4924

LEATHER

A. Barra of Italy
417 Park Avenue
New York, NY 10022
(212) 355-5881

Berman Leather Co.
145 South Street
Boston, MA 02111
(617) 425-0870

Dolfinger's Inc.
325 West Walnut Street
Louisville, KY 40202
(502) 893-3634

Salvatore Ferragamo
717 Fifth Avenue
New York, NY 10022
(212) 759-3822

Gucci Shops, Inc.
713 North Michigan Avenue
Chicago, IL 60611
(312) 664-5504

685 and 689 Fifth Avenue
New York, NY 10022
(212) 826-2600

256 Worth Avenue
Palm Beach, FL 33480
(306) 655-6955

Desert Fashion Plaza
123 North Palm Canyon Drive
Palm Springs, CA 92262
(619) 322-0880

Rose Lash/Corrine Travis
58 East 55th Street
New York, NY 10022
(212) 759-6213

LIGHTING

Arteluce
595 Madison Avenue
New York, NY 10022
(212) 644-0400

Artemide
The Merchandise Mart
Suite 851
Chicago, IL 60654
(312) 644-0510

150 East 58th Street
New York, NY 10155
(212) 980-0710

Bieffeplast U.S.A. Inc.
300 West 55th Street
New York, NY 10019
(212) 541-6654

Mel Brown International
5840 South Figuero Street
Los Angeles, CA 90003
(213) 686-2371

Casella Lighting Co.
111 Rhode Island Street
San Francisco, CA 94103
(415) 626-9600

Castel Chandeliers & Lighting Co.,
   Inc.
12318 Ventura Boulevard
Studio City, CA 91604
(213) 766-4218

Collezione Simon Ltd.
22 Madison Avenue
Paramus, NJ 07652
(201) 587-9013

Interior Design Ltd.
The Merchandise Mart
Chicago, IL 60654
(312) 467-6076

Ipi Lighting
315 East 62nd Street
New York, NY 10021
(212) 838-9200
Luceplan lighting

Lighting Associates Inc.
306 East 63rd Street
New York, NY 10021
(212) 751-0515

Lumen Design Co.
P.O. Box 5172
Beverly Hills, CA 90210
(213) 855-1185

MEDIA

Attenzione
Subscriptions Services Dept.
P.O. Box 1917
Merion, OH 43306

The Galling Report on Italy
4 East 70th Street
New York, NY 10021
(212) 517-7782

Il Progresso Italo-Americano
15 Bland Street
Emerson, NJ 07630
(212) 695-5500
(201) 262-2239

L'Agenda
26 Court Street
Brooklyn, NY 11242
(718) 875-0580

La Stampa
565 Fifth Avenue
New York, NY 10017
(212) 363-4741

MUSEUMS & GALLERIES

Art Originals
2346 Frankfort Avenue
Louisville, KY 40206
(502) 895-9933

Indianapolis Museum of Art
1200 West 38th Street
Indianapolis, IN 46208
(317) 923-1221
Italian 18th-century decorative art

Phyllis Lucas and Camilla Lucas
   Gallery
881 Second Avenue
New York, NY 10022
(212) 755-1516
original lithographs

The Metropolitan Museum of Art
Fifth Avenue at 81st Street
New York, NY 10028
(212) 535-7710
general collection

Museo Italo-Americano
512 Union Street
San Francisco, CA 94133
(415) 982-6306

Museum of Fine Arts
465 Huntington Avenue
Boston, MA 02215
(617) 267-9300

The National Gallery of Art
Sixth Street & Constitution Avenue
   NW
Washington, DC 20565
(202) 737-4215
*works by da Vinci, Raphael, Fra
   Filippo Lippi, among others*

Nelson Gallery of Art and Atkins
   Museum
4525 Oak Street
Kansas City, MO 64111
(816) 561-4000
Roman sculpture

New Orleans Museum of Art
City Park
New Orleans, LA 70119
(504) 488-2631
Renaissance masterpieces

Philadephia Museum of Art
26th & Benjamin Franklin Parkway
Philadelphia, PA 19101
(215) 763–8100
all periods

Sperone Westwater Fischer
142 Greene Street
New York, NY 10012
(212) 431–3685

Timken Art Gallery
Plaza de Panama
Balboa Park
San Diego, CA 92101
(619) 239–5548
Renaissance art

Victoria Mansion
109 Danforth Street
Portland, ME 04101
(207) 772–4841
an Italian villa

Walters Art Gallery
Charles & Centre Streets
Baltimore, MD 21201–5185
(301) 547–9000

Yale University Art Gallery
1111 Chapel Street
New Haven, CT 06520
(203) 436–0574
ancient Roman art and architecture

SHOES

Giorgio Armani
576 Fifth Avenue
New York, NY 10036
(212) 869–0499

Beltrami, Inc.
711 Fifth Avenue
New York, NY 10022
(212) 838–4101

Bergdorf Goodman
Delman Shoe Salon
754 Fifth Avenue
New York, NY 10022
(212) 872–8882

Boccioni Inc.
958 Third Avenue
New York, NY 10022
(212) 319–6580

Botticelli Shoes
666 Fifth Avenue
New York, NY 10022
(212) 582–2984

Andrea Carrano, Ltd.
677 Fifth Avenue
New York, NY 10022
(212) 752–6111

City Slicker
164 Monroe
Detroit, MI 48226
(313) 963–1963

Henri Devignon
45 West 34th Street
New York, NY 10001
(212) 594–1017

Salvatore Ferragamo
717 Fifth Avenue
New York, NY 10022
(212) 759–3822

Fratelli Rosseti N.Y. Ltd.
601 Madison Avenue
New York, NY 10022
(212) 888–5107

Nino Gabriele Shoes
169 East 60th Street
New York, NY 10022
(212) 421–3250

Garolini Shoes
717 Fifth Avenue
New York, NY 10022
(212) 223–4640 *showroom*
(800) 523–8948 (*for locations
    around country*)

Giorgio
2151 Lemoine Avenue
Fort Lee, NJ 07024
(201) 585–9284

Giovanna
202 East 60th Street
New York, NY 10022
(212) 758–1200

The Glass Slipper
139 Orchard Street
New York, NY 10002
(212) 598–4230

Gucci
689 Fifth Avenue
New York, NY 10022
(212) 826–2600

I. Miller Shoes
734 Fifth Avenue
New York, NY 10019
(212) 581–0062

Rose Lash/Corrine Travis
58 East 55th Street
New York, NY 10022
(212) 759–6213

Mr. Sid, Inc.
1211 Centre Street
Newton, MA 02195
(617) 969–4540

Vittorio Ricci
645 Madison Avenue
(212) 688–9044

Santini and Dominici
697 Madison Avenue
New York, NY 10021
(212) 838–1835

Serendipity
8401 Germantown Avenue
Philadelphia, PA 19118
(215) 242–1111

Strega
1505 Walnut Street
Philadelphia, PA 19102
(215) 564–5932

Tanino Cresci
703 Madison Avenue
New York, NY 10021
(212) 308–7778

SILVER

Bloomingdales
1000 Third Avenue
New York, NY 10022
(212) 355–5900
Ricci silverware

Buccellati, Inc.
46 East 57th Street
New York, NY 10022
(212) 308–2900

Joan Cook Co.
3200 Southeast 14th Avenue
Fort Lauderdale, FL 33316
(305) 761–1600

Fortunoff Fine Jewelry & Silverware
681 Fifth Avenue
New York, NY 10022
(212) 758–6660

TEXTILES

Ad Hoc Softwares
410 West Broadway
New York, NY 10012
(212) 925–2652

Amrose Art Linens Inc.
22 West 19th Street
New York, NY 10011–4204
(212) 206–7632

Frette Fine Linens
787 Madison Avenue
New York, NY 10021
(212) 988–5221

Handicraft from Europe
454 Colonna
P.O. Box 372
Sausalito, CA 94966
(415) 332–1633

Pratesi Linens, Inc.
829 Madison Avenue
New York, NY 10021
(212) 288–2315

TILE

Domus Corporation
9734 Hayne Boulevard
New Orleans, LA 70127
(504) 242-5480

Hastings II Bagno Collection
201 East 57th Street
New York, NY 10022
(212) 755-2710

Plain & Fancy Tile Company
714 East Green Street
Pasadena, CA 91101
(213) 577-2830
hand-painted imports

Smolka Co. Inc.
182 Madison Avenue
New York, NY 10016
(212) 679-2700

TRADE ORGANIZATIONS

Italian Fashion Center
499 Park Avenue
New York, NY 10022
(212) 980-1500

Italian Tile Center
499 Park Avenue
New York, NY 10022
(212) 980-8866

Italian Trade Center
499 Park Avenue
New York, NY 10022
(212) 371-8989

Italian Trade Commission
499 Park Avenue
New York, NY 10022
(212) 980-1500

Italian Wine & Food Institute
160 East 65th Street
New York, NY 10021
(212) 371-2350

Wines of Tuscany
Suite 2507
One World Trade Center
New York, NY 10048

TRAVEL

Alitalia Airlines
666 Fifth Avenue
New York, NY 10022
(212) 903-3300

Italian Government Travel Office
500 North Michigan Avenue
Chicago, IL 60611
(312) 644-0990

630 Fifth Avenue
New York, NY 10111
(212) 245-4822

360 Post Street
San Francisco, CA 94108
(415) 392-6206

Italian Line
26 Broadway
New York, NY 10004
(212) 422-3500

Italian Travel Company
666 Fifth Avenue
New York, NY 10103
(212) 397-9300

ENGLAND

CARS

Alfa Romeo (GB) Limited
Geron Way
London NW2 6LW
(01) 450-9191

Ferraris of Cricklewood Limited
220 Cricklewood
Broadway
London NW2 3DT
(01) 452-2234

London Sales
Edgeware Road
London NW2 6LX
(01) 450-8641

CERAMICS

Casa Pupo
58-60 Pimlico Road
London SW1
(01) 730-7111

Italian Porcelain & Ceramic
144 Station Road
London E4
(01) 529-6400

FASHION

Women's

Giorgio Armani
26 South Molton Street
London W1
(01) 491-7605

Browns
23-27 South Molton Street
London W1
(01) 491-7833

Dee Dawson
5 Thayer Street
London W1
(01) 935-7527

Elle
4 New Bond Street
London SW3
(01) 629-4441

Fendi
37 Sloane Street
London SW1
(01) 235-9966

Ferragamo Ltd.
24 Old Bond Street
London W1
(01) 629-5007

Ferré
80/A Brompton Road
London SW1

37/B Brook Street
London W1

Genny
Knights Arcade
Brompton Road
London SW1

Fiorucci
133 New Bond Street
London SW1
(01) 499-3499

Harrods
87-135 Brompton Road
London SW1
(01) 730-1234

L'Expressions Utile
32 Englands Lane
Hampstead
(01) 586-3931

Piero de Monzi
68-72 Fulham Road
London SW3
(01) 581-4247

Regine
43 New Bond Street
London W1
(01) 499-0788
Complice, Versace, Valentino

Valentino Boutique
160 New Bond Street
London W1
(01) 629-3181

Gianni Versace
35 Brook Street
London W1
(01) 409-1670

FASHION

Men's

Giorgio Armani
26 South Molton Street
London W1
(O1) 495–7605

Browns
23-27 South Molton Street
London W1
(O1) 629–4049

Ebony
45 South Molton Street
London W1
(O1) 408–1247

Elle (Uomo) Ltd.
8 Duke Street
London W1M
(O1) 935–1491

Harrods
87-135 Brompton Road
London SW1
(O1) 730–1234

Jones
129 King's Road
London SW3
(O1) 352–5323
suits

Piero de Monzi
68-72 Fulham Road
London SW3
(O1) 581–4247

Tariq
24 St. Christopher's Place
London W1
(O1) 935–6255

Gianni Versace
35 Brook Street
London W1
(O1) 409–1670

Vincii
60 Jermynn Street
London W1
(O1) 493–4651

Woodhouse
99 Oxford Street
London W1
(O1) 437–2809

FASHION

Children's

Little Horrors
16 Cheval Place
London SW7
(O1) 589–5289

Mome
27 Harrington Road
London SW7
(O1) 589–8306

Pomme d'Api
154b Walton Street
London SW3
(O1) 584–1596

Zero Four
53 South Molton Street
London W1
(O1) 493–4920

FOOD & COOKING SUPPLIES

Fortnum and Mason
181 Piccadilly
London W1
(O1) 734–8080

Fratelli Camisa
1A Berwick Street
London W1
(O1) 437–7120

Harrods Pantry
87–135 Brompton Road
London SW1
(O1) 730–1234

Hobbs
3 Garrick Street
London WC2
(O1) 240–5653

29 South Audley Street
London W1
(O1) 409–1048

Justerini and Brooks
61 St. James Street
London SW1
(O1) 493–8721

Marine Ices
8 Haverstock Hill
London NW3
(O1) 485–8898

Neal's Yard Wholefood Warehouse
2 Neal's Yard
London SC2
(O1) 240–1154

Parmigiani
36a Old Compton Street
London W1
(O1) 437–4728

FURNISHINGS

J.D. Beardmore & Co. Ltd.
Field End Road
Ruislip, Middlesex
(O1) 864–6811

B.F.E. Ltd.
16-17 Lower Square
Isleworth, Middlesex
London TW7 6BW
(O1) 847–0440

Breslew & Partners
11 Chelwood Gardens
Kew, Richmond
Surrey TW9 4JG
Pottrovna furniture importers

Class International
31 Sloane Street
Knightsbridge
London SW1
(O1) 235–8452

D.D. Flicker Interiors Ltd.
17 Rosemont Road
London NW36 8NG
Estel furniture

Forma Furniture
149 Upper Richmond Road
London SW15
(O1) 788–2538

Hamilton's International Ltd.
492-494 Bromley Road
Downham, Bromley, Kent
Elam furniture importers

Pour La Maison
16 Sloane Street
London SW1

Rod Morton International Furniture
Ripley Castle Courtyard
Ripley, Harrogate
North Yorkshire HG3 3AY
(O423) 771587
importer

Shop & Store Planners Ltd.
Almeida Street
London N1
(O1) 226–8686

WCB Plastics Unlimited
Road One
Industrial Estate
Winsford, Cheshire
(O60) 655–3921
importer

GENERAL ORGANIZATIONS

British-Italian Society
Kensington Brks
Kensington Church Street
London W8
(O1) 937–1644

Italian Chamber of Commerce for
  Great Britain
Walmar House
Regent Street
London W1
(O1) 637–3153

Italian Consulate General
38 Eaton Place
London SW1
(O1) 235–9371

Italian Design & International
   Contractors
47 Eastcastle Street
London W1N 9DJ
(O1) 580–7626

Italian Institute of Culture
39 Belgrave Square
London SW1X 8NX
(O1) 236–1461

Italian News Agency
Communications House
Gough Square
London EC4
(O1) 353–3978

Italian Trade Centre
37 Sackville Street
London W1
(O1) 734–2412
(O1) 439–2991 *wine enquiries*

Italian Wine Agencies
Great Britain House
High Road
London NW1O
(O1) 459–1515

LEATHER

Gucci
27 Old Bond Street
London W1
(O1) 629–2716

Janet Ibbotson
7 Pond Place
London SW3
(O1) 584–2856

LIGHTING

Aram Design Ltd.
3 Kean Street
Covent Garden
London WC2B 4AT
(O1) 636–6568
Luceplan lighting

Artemide
17–19 Neal Street
Covent Garden
London WC2H 9PU
(O1) 836–6953

Atrium
113 St. Peter's Street
St. Albans, Herts AL1 3ET
(O727) 37356

Flos Ltd.
Heath Hall
Heath Wakefield
WF1 5SL
(O924) 366–4467

Forma Lighting Ltd.
Unit 3
Mitcham Industrial Estate
85 Streatham Road
Mitcham, Surrey CR4 2AP

149 Upper Richmond Road
London SW15 2TX
(O1) 788–2538

MUSEUMS & GALLERIES

Agnew
43 Old Bond Street
London W1
(O1) 629–6176

British Museum
Great Russell Street
Bloomsbury
London WC1B 3DG
(O1) 636–1555
Roman artifacts, 16th-century works

National Gallery
Trafalgar Square
London WC2N 5DN
(O1) 839–3321

Walker Art Gallery
William Brown Street
Liverpool, Merseyside
L3 8EL
(O51) 227–5234
early Italian collection

Wallace Collection
Hertford House
Manchester Square
London W1M 6BN
(O1) 935–O687
Italian objets d'art

Wildenstein
147 New Bond Street
London W1
(O1) 629–O602

SHOES

Browns
23 South Molton Street
London W1
(O1) 629–4049

Celine
28 New Bond Street
London W1
(O1) 493–9000

Salvatore Ferragamo
24 Old Bond Street
London W1
(O1) 629–5007

Gucci
27 Old Bond Street
London W1
(O1) 629–2717

Hobbs
47 South Molton Street
London W1
(O1) 629–O750

Bruno Magli
123 New Bond Street
London W1X 9AB
(O1) 493–O733

2O7A Sloane Street
London

Piero de Monzi
68–72 Fulham Road
London SW3
(O1) 582–4247

Rider
231 Kings Road
London SW3
(O1) 352–3198

Rossetti
177 New Bond Street
London W1
(O1) 491–7066

Russell & Bromley
24-25 New Bond Street
London W1
(O1) 491–7066

Wardrobe
17 Chiltern Street
London W1
(O1) 935–4086

3 Grosvenor Street
London W1
(O1) 629–7O44

TEXTILES

Frette Ltd.
98 New Bond Street
London W1
(O1) 629–5517

Vantona International Linen
2O Brook Street
London W1
(O1) 629–5000

The White House
51-52 New Bond Street
London W1
(O1) 629–3521

TRAVEL

Alitalia
27 Piccadilly
London W1
(01) 759–2510

Citalia
Department HQ
Marco Polo House
3-5 Lansdowne Road
Croydon CR91LL

Italian International Travel Centre
Ltd.
33 Old Compton Street
London W1
(01) 434–2250

CANADA

FASHION

The Bay
2 Bloor Street East
Toronto, Ontario
M4W 3H7
(416) 964–5511
Biagiotti

Benetton
1216 St. Clair West
Toronto, Ontario
M6E 1B4
(416) 657–1258

663 Yonge Street
M4Y 2A4
(416) 967–0087

Chez Catherine
20A Hazelton Avenue
Hazelton Lanes
Toronto, Ontario
M5R 2E2
(416) 967–5666
Biagiotti, Ferré, Versace, Valentino

Creeds
45 Bloor Street West
Toronto, Ontario
M4W 1A4
(416) 923–1000
Armani, Krizia, Valentino

Dorrit
47 Avenue Road
Toronto, Ontario
M5R 2G3
(416) 920–1940
Byblos

Genevieve Boutique
1010 Yorkville Avenue
Toronto, Ontario
M4W 1L2
(416) 964–0525

Hazelton Lanes
55 Avenue Road
Toronto, Ontario
M5R 3L2
(416) 968–8600

Holt Renfrew & Company, Ltd.
The Holt Renfrew Centre
50 Bloor Street West
Toronto, Ontario
M4W 3L8
(416) 922–2333
other locations: Montreal, Quebec,
Winnipeg, Vancouver, Edmonton,
Calgary; collections: Armani,
Fendi, Gianfranco Ferré, Genny,
Valentino, Byblos

FURNISHINGS

AREA Designs
334 King Street East
Toronto, Ontario
M5A 1K8
(416) 367–5850
Alessi designs

Artemide Ltd.
2408 De La Province
Longueuil, Quebec
J4G 1G1
(514) 651–9133

Au Courant
4201 Ouest Rue Catherine
Montreal, Quebec
H3Z 1T6
(514) 932–3415

Chateau d'Aujourd'hui
1125 Boulevard Saint Martin
Chomedey-Laval , Quebec
H7S 1M8
(514) 382–4710
Brunati furniture

Novella
P.O. Box 239
Henryville, Quebec
J0J 1E0
(418) 651–9133
Venini glass

Pratesi Linens, Inc.
1448 Sherbrooke Street West
Montreal, Quebec
H3G 1K4
(514) 285–8909

Triede Design Inc.
296 Ouest Rue St. Paul
Montreal, Quebec
H27 2A3
(514) 288–0063
Arteluce

GENERAL ORGANIZATIONS

The Canadian Society for Italian
Studies
c/o Department of Modern
Languages
University of Ottawa
Ottawa, Ontario
K1N 6N5
(613) 231–5471

Italian Chamber of Commerce of
Montreal
1255 Phillips Square
Suite 1109
Montreal, Quebec
H3B 361
(514) 866–0070

Italian Chamber of Commerce of
Toronto
159 Bay Street
Suite 313
Toronto, Ontario
M5J 1J7
(416) 364–6551

Italian Cultural Institute
496 Huron Street
Toronto, Ontario
M5R 2R3
(416) 921–3802

Italian Government Travel Office
N–3 Place Ville Marie
Montreal, Quebec
H3B 2E3
(514) 866–7667

Italo-Canadian Cultural Association
6050 Almon Street
Halifax, Nova Scotia
B3K 1T8
(902) 455–9304

SHOES

Chez Catherine
20A Hazelton Avenue
Hazelton Lanes
Toronto, Ontario
M5R 2E2
(416) 967–5666

Givan Shoes
1240 Bay Street
Toronto, Ontario
M5R 2A7
(416) 923–2272

Tara Shoes
20 Bloor Street East
Toronto, Ontario
M4W 1A7
(416) 964–8996

Index

Page numbers in italics refer to captions and illustrations.

Photography Credits

Courtesy of Arteluce: p. 28 (*l*)

Art Resource, New York: p. 128–129, 130, 131, 134–135, 136, 137, 160, 161 (*top*),163

Courtesy of B + B Italia: p. 17, 26–27, 28 (*r*), 29

Gabriele Basilico (Editrice Abitare Segesta): p. 14–15, 16 (*top*)

Courtesy of Laura Biagiotti Eyewear for Private Eyes, New York: p. 83

Alessandro Buzzanca: p. 30–31, 33

Bruce Caines: p. 76 (*center*), 78, 81, 82 (*l*), 84, 85, 88–89, 90;
  Models: p. 76, Walter Bryant/Bonnie Kay Model Management;
    p. 78, Angela Gili/Elite Model Management, Jared Moore/Bonnie Kay
    Model Management; p. 81, Doug Spitz/Bonnie Kay Model Management;
    p. 82, Mila/Bonnie Kay Model Management; p. 90, Courtesy of Carrano

Enrico Cattaneo (Editrice Abitare Segesta): p. 15 (*r*)

Tony Cenicola: p. 96, 166–167, 174–175

Courtesy of Christie's Colour Library, London: p. 144–145

Courtesy of Christie's East, New York: p. 150

Courtesy of Christie, Manson & Woods International Inc., New York: p. 35

Courtesy of Christie's South Kensington, London: p. 86 (*l*)

Margaret Courtney-Clarke: p. 8–9, 12–13, 32, 34, 36–37, 43, 48 (*top l*), 56 (*l*), 57
  (*bottom*), 60, 61 (*bottom*), 62, 63, 64 (*bottom*), 65, 66–67, 68, 69, 70 (*top l*),
  74–75, 76 (*l*), 80, 86, 87, 94–95, 97, 100, 107, 108, 132–133, 149 (*l*), 151,
  152–153, 161 (*bottom*), 162, 164, 165, 170, 171, 174 (*l*)

John Deane: p. 98

Louis De Pootere: p. 18–19

The Design Council, London: p. 14 (*l*), 16 (*bottom*), 22

John Dominis (Wheeler Pictures, New York): p. 56–57, 64 (*top*), 71 (*insert*)

Karen Eisenstadt: p. 61 (*top*)

W. Filiputti: p. 184

Maria Pia Giarre: p. 79, 109, 148, 154–155, 176–177, 178

Leslie Gill © Frances McLaughlin-Gill: p. 139, 141

Courtesy of Gucci, New York: p. 76–77, 90–91

Courtesy of Martina Hamilton, New York: p. 122–123

Rainer Krause: Courtesy of Peter Frank, Nr photographer: p. 23

Guglielmo Mairani (Grazie Neri, Milan): p. 98–99, 103 (*r*), 105, 106, 114–115,
  179, 182, 185, 187, 188

Marciani: p. 104

Silvia Massotti: p. 119

Joe McNally (Wheeler Pictures, New York): p. 149 (*r*)

Courtesy of Memphis, Milan: p. 20, 21

National Film Archive, London: p. 140, 142–143

© National Gallery of Art, Washington, DC: p. 147

F. Piersanti: p. 101, 102, 110–111, 112, 113, 116–117, 118

Jonathon E. Pite: p. 54–55, 59

Maurizio Plutino (Grazie Neri, Milan): p. 181

Ornella Sancassani (Editrice Abitare Segesta): p. 31 (*insert*)

Courtesy of Smithsonian Institution, photo no. 52202: p. 156–157

Paul Solomon (Wheeler Pictures, New York): p. 52–53, 55 (*insert*), 58, 62 (*insert*),
  82–83, 146, 168–169, 172–173, 180

Mario Tedeschi: p. 38, 39, 40, 42, 44, 45, 46, 47, 48 (*r*), 49, 50, 51

Peter Tenzer (Wheeler Pictures, New York): p. 70–71

Courtesy of Watson/Hague/Einstein, Inc., Los Angeles: p. 24, 25

Courtesy of Sperone Westwater, New York: p. 120, 121, 124 (Zindman/Fremont
  photo), 125, 126, 127 (Zindman/Fremont photo)

Courtesy of Wintering Communications: p. 158, 159